A Life Behind Bars

By TJ Carmody

A LIFE BEHIND BARS

No part of this publication may be reproduced, stored in a retrieval system, or transmitted in any form or by any means without the prior written specific permission of the publisher.

DEDICATIONS

To my Mother: Miss Muvvy
<u>October 7, 1917 to May 8, 2010</u>
She is the one who told me to write the
book, and she also came up with the title!

To my two boys: R.T. and Patrick
And to their mother, Wendy,
who witnessed a few stories

To my wife: Sue, who has seen it all!
And to her support, with
the line: "Finish the Book!"

To Sue's kids: Ryan, Jeffery & Kelly,
who I consider as my own kids!

To my brothers, sisters, nieces and nephews,
who have always supported me!

To my Grandchildren: Addison and Mera! Love from Grampy!

Ray Lambert who helped me
put these stories on paper!

~ DISCLAIMER ~

These are my stories. They have been fine-tuned over the years. They've been told in my bars and at parties and on the golf course – and, any other place where someone would listen to them!

They are true stories as far as I am concerned! Well, at least what's very true is that this is the way I remember them!

Some people reading this book might think that it is them in one or another story – or – may have a different view of the story.

If you think it is you? Well, it might be … or it might not be!

As far as the truth of the stories?

If you disagree? Write your own damn book!

A note from *Suzanne Carmody:*

TJ asked me one time, "Can't you take a joke?"

My reply to him was, "I'm dating you, aren't I?"

'-- *Suzanne Carmody*

CONTACT:

You can contact TJ at:

email: Tjcarmody17@yahoo.com

Facebook: TJCARMODY

QUICK INTRODUCTION

By TJ

Everyone looks at their life and wonders what they would have done differently. If they changed something, would they have been more successful, made more money, been more popular, done better in love?

They say hindsight is 20/20.

At 62 going on 63 I wonder the same things. If I went to a different college? Took a different job? If I had been born into a different family, maybe one with a summer house on Cape Cod and a winter house in Florida?

I know that I would never have been a snob if I was born to a family with privilege.

Just kidding!

My mother was the one who has kept pressing me to write a book. I kept telling her, "No way!"

A guy who cheated his way through English in high school is going to write a book? Plus, what the hell do I have to write a book about? For years, though, she kept putting the idea in my head. One day she tells me that she has the title for my book.

"Okay mom. What is the title of my book?"

Her reply was, "My Life Behind Bars."

Not bad. But I am not ready yet.

*Note to the reader: Someone already has that book title, so my book title is **A** Life Behind Bars.*

RAY WAS RIGHT

In high school I had a guidance counselor who used to be a priest. His name was Ray.

Ray looked at my transcripts with me and figured out the only things I was good at in school was sports, girls and partying. It might be wise, he thought, if I went into the family business and became a funeral director. I was thinking of playing basketball for Norte Dame ... but at 5'10" and white, with grades so bad I was lucky they let me graduate? Maybe Ray was right.

Fast forward a bunch of years to Carmody's on Main Street in Bennington, Vermont. In comes Ray. He's teaching a couple of classes at the community college down the street. He stops in every once and a while for a drink and a cigar before he heads home.

We catch up on each other's lives. I start telling Ray about some of my crazy stories in the funeral business and the bar business. I tell him my mother thinks I should write a book and has the title.

One night Ray comes in and hands me a small tape recorder, telling me "When you get a few cocktails into you and start telling these stories, start the recorder! I want to help you write the book." I don't know what happened to the tape recorder! Unfortunately, I never had it with me when I had a few and started telling stories.

Fast forward again. I'm in Stuart, Florida. I reflect on my life and start thinking about all the things I have done, the good times I have had, the family and friends I have, the people I have affected and raised money for. I haven't done too badly.

So I start writing the "Book." I get a lot of stories done, but don't know where to go next.

Out of the clear blue, I remember Ray. After doing research and trying to find out where he is and if he is still alive, I call a telephone number I have found just before Christmas of 2015.

I leave a message, saying, "Uh, this is TJ Carmody. I am trying to find Ray. He was my guidance counselor in high school. If this is Ray, could you please call me back?"

I was happy I got voicemail. I didn't want to talk to anyone if this wasn't Ray's number, or if something had happened to him.

A couple of hours later my cell rings. I'm at the mall with Sue, Christmas shopping. Holy Shit! It's Ray!

Ray and I talk. I tell him I am writing the book. He is very enthusiastic about it and is willing to help -- so the book writing journey begins!

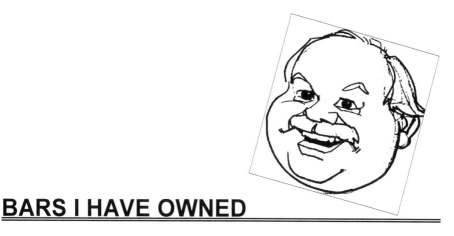

BARS I HAVE OWNED

*I've owned or have been a partner in a few bars and
restaurants over the years. Let me start with the first and
end up with the last:*

PT'S PUB, BENNINGTON, VERMONT: I had moved from
Florida to Bennington to be closer to my boys. I got a job
selling beer and wine in Bennington County.

There's this old bar in Bennington where the other
salesmen and I would go once a week for a few beers.

The bar had been there for years. It used to open early
in the morning, and as a kid you would go by and see
every garbage truck in the area parked out front. The
guys were in there drinking, after making their early
rounds of collecting garbage. The place always had a bad
reputation.

It was then owned by a nephew of the original owner,
and he wanted to sell it.

Well I started to think I could turn this place around with the experience that I had in Florida.

I didn't have any money, so I started looking for a backer among family and friends. But ... nobody I talked to seemed interested in becoming a partner in a dive bar in Bennington, Vermont.

I happened to make contact with a former customer at Danny's in Fort Lauderdale, Florida. He asked me what I was doing, so I told him I was selling beer and was trying to buy this bar.

He told me that he was going back and forth between Florida and Vermont quite a bit, and that he would be interested in investing in the bar.

Here's how that went: So a couple of weeks later, I show my former bar customer the bar and go out to dinner with him to discuss the proposition.

He is very interested. I tell him I have moved back to Vermont to be closer to my two boys and I don't want to do anything to jeopardize that. I had heard he made his money selling cocaine. He says that is just a rumor, and that his money comes from a patent he has on washable wallpaper.

I wanted to do a deal, so I put the blinders on, and I go with it.

We purchase the bar and do some minor renovations and painting. We get some good press in the local paper, and open up.

Things are rocking! We turn the place around. We have entertainment on Friday and Saturdays and crazy promotions during the week.

The bar is on a corner lot and is built right up to the side walk, but in the back of the bar there's an **L** shaped parking area that is never used. I come up with the idea of putting a volleyball court back there.

Not knowing shit about volleyball, the only thing I knew is that there's a bar in Manchester with a couple of courts ... and they are very busy.

Why not Bennington?

So we proceed to build the court. A friend of mine in the construction business helps us build the court.

There's no web back then, so I go to the library and get a book about volleyball. Our court is going to be smaller than a regulation court. Who cares? I get flyers out about starting a couple of leagues. I hold the first meeting and the place is packed!

The first year we have 24 teams of six, playing volleyball Monday through Thursday. With entertainment on Friday and Saturday, the little bar is rocking six days a week!

My partner and I are getting along great. The money is good and everyone is having a good time. We roll along, have a great summer and fall, and get through the winter. With spring coming, I take a look at the back lot where the volleyball court is and think I might be able to squeeze in another court. We put in the other court and get started with volleyball in the spring. This time we have 48 teams playing! We are going to rock this summer!

Then it happens.

My partner gets caught with 8 ½ oz. of coke. They search his house, and by the way, I also live there.

They just ripped everything apart. He disappears! I'm left running the bar, not knowing what's going to happen. The state of Vermont wants to take our liquor license and close us down. I get an attorney and we go up to Rutland to go before the liquor board. I am armed with letters from the community saying what a good job we are doing in Bennington, and that we should stay open at least until the case is settled and everyone figures out what is going on.

We are in front of the liquor board and who would come out of the wood work? None other than my partner and his attorney!

He tries to pin the drugs on to me. The State tells us we can stay open, but my partner can't be involved in the business until his drug case is settled. I tell my attorney that we should walk away and let my partner have it all, because he will never get a liquor license.

The lawyer suggests to me that we should hang in there. He thinks it will work out fine.

Okay, so we will do it his way.

I try to talk to my partner, but he wants no part of it and starts accusing me of screwing him! Holy Shit! You are the one who has been dealing coke, not me!

We leave Montpelier with our deal with the state, and I go to the bar the next morning, doing the paper work up in the office.

Who should show up? My partner's lawyer walks in, holding a letter stating that as majority owner, my partner is relieving me of my duties, and stating that I must vacate the premises.

I contact my lawyer and meet with him. Everything is legit and I'm out of there! And I am off to Florida to do bar number 2.

SHARKEY'S TROPICAL GRILLE: The day I lose P.T.'s Pub a friend of mine arrives from Stuart, Florida. He and I are playing golf.

He tells me he wants me to be his partner in a waterfront restaurant in Stuart. Awesome! Going from a dive to a waterfront bar? Let's go!

I pack up the car and head to Stuart. The restaurant we are looking at is right on the waterfront in downtown Stuart. Beautiful location, but it needs some work.

My partner and I are examining the place when Florida gets one of those afternoon summer showers. The water is flowing right into the restaurant! The leaky roof doesn't faze my partner, though.

He says, "We'll just have the landlord fix it."

Okay!

A couple of days later we are in Palm Beach for a bankruptcy hearing for the restaurant owners, who were in the building before us. The landlord is at the hearing.

My partner goes over to him and tells him that we would like to rent the restaurant. The landlord looks at my partner and tells him there is "no fucking way" he would lease the restaurant to him!

Well, that went over real well! Now what do we do?

On our way back to Stuart, my partner tells me there is another place he is looking at. He asks me if I would be interested in the other place. Well, I am in Florida. I might just as well.

And that's how we ended up opening Sharkey's Tropical Grill.

We purchased four big fish tanks and filled them with tropical fish, including two sharks that we had flown in from California. The shark delivery got delayed in Houston, and the sharks arrived about an hour before the grand opening.

We got the sharks in the tanks, and about an hour later one of the sharks is floating at the top of the tank, upside down.

Today's Special: Shark soup!

I lasted less than a year at Sharkey's. I missed my boys and moved back to Vermont ... and to bar number 3.

T.J. O'CARMODY'S HOOSICK FALLS NY: After Sharkey's, I moved back to Bennington. I did a little bartending and worked at a Funeral Home.

One day I hear about a bar in Hoosick Falls that the owner wants to sell.

I meet up with him and we work out a deal where I will lease the place for two years with an option to buy it. There were no renovations.

We sign the papers on a Friday morning and I am open that night. It's a late late night bar. We are open until 4 a.m. Friday and Saturday nights.

I have a lot fun at this little bar and do some of my craziest promotions there.

I also have volleyball again.

There is a vacant lot across the street owned by the railroad. I think I could buy the lot and put in a couple of volleyball courts. So I call the railroad to see how much they want for the lot. They tell me they want $20,000 for the lot. I ask if they will take $15,000.

They reply, "Hey kid, we are the railroad. We don't care if we sell it or not. If you want it, it's $20,000."

Do I know how to close a deal! Wow!

We buy the lot, put two courts in, and it takes off. The old P.T.'s Pub is closed, so I get all the volleyball players from Bennington. We have a great summer and things are rocking.

The next summer, P.T.'s reopens with new owners. They restart volleyball. It cuts my leagues in half. At this time, business is slow. People are afraid of driving at 4 a.m. because the cops are stopping everyone.

I decide that I don't want to buy the place, and won't renew the lease. I sell the lot with the courts, and close down the bar with an Irish Wake!

After Hoosick, I moved to Myrtle Beach for about nine months, but I wanted to get back to Vermont.

Another small bar was in foreclosure in Bennington. I thought I could pick it up cheap, so I drove 24-hours straight from Vermont to Stuart, Florida and convinced my brother to back me.

I called my attorney, from Jacksonville, Florida, and drove straight back early in the morning to make the offer. I got a little shut eye, woke up, and called my attorney to ask him if everything was all set.

He told me I had lost the deal. Someone else made the same offer as I did, but told the bank they could sell off the equipment. The bank, being a bank, figured it would get another two grand ... and took that deal. I was left out in cold.

From there?

That night I run into a customer who used to come into P.T.'s Pub. He owns two bars on Long Island. He asks me what I am up to, and I tell about losing the deal. He looks at me and says, "Why don't we do a deal together? You find a place and I will be your partner."

Well, the next day we look at a place in North Bennington, and that's the beginning of T.J.'s and Mikes Place.

We do a bunch of renovations -- new bathrooms, new kitchen, and a couple of other things.

We finally get the place ready to open and my partner sends up one of his chefs from Long Island to run the kitchen.

The place does great and we have lots of fun there. After about three and a half years, I have an opportunity to open a place downtown Bennington again.

The partners aren't too happy that I'm leaving, but this is the place I want.

CARMODY'S BENNINGTON, VERMONT: So we close on Carmody's in November, 1998, and open up January.

We do major renovations. You can see from the front window all the way to the back wall. The only standing piece is the ice machine. During renovations, people buy gift certificates for Christmas. I stand in the sawdust with my Santa hat on Christmas Eve.

It feels so good that people are that excited about us opening up. We last close to 14 years and have some great times there.

CARMODY'S STUART, FLORIDA: Screwing around on the internet, I find a liquor license for Martin County, Florida where the city of Stuart is located. I purchase the license and find a strip mall with a couple of vacant stores.

We lease the spaces, tear down the wall and build Carmody's South.

Business is good, but it was very difficult running two places 1500 miles apart. We sell the business after operating it for three years.

CARMODY'S WEST HOOSICK, NEW YORK: This is a late night bar on the state line between Vermont and New York.

In New York, you can stay open till 4 a.m., and you can do more liquor promotions.

The place does well, but is too close to Bennington, because I'm just splitting my customer base. We close the place down and try to sell it, but there are no buyers. So I hang on to it.

PLOUGHMAN'S PUB HOOSICK NY: This was a reincarnation of Carmody's West. I reopened after closing Carmody's in downtown Bennington. I tried to remain in the area and to keep doing what I love to do.

The State of Vermont had put in a bypass around Bennington. This took away all the tourists that used to go through Bennington. I couldn't get the traffic off the new road either at Carmody's in Bennington or at Ploughman's Pub.

We closed down. It was my last hurrah.

Here are stories of my life behind bars and caskets ...

Story #2

HARPERS & CORAL SPRINGS

My first bartending job was at Harpers Pub and Wet Goods, in Stuart, Farida. My next job in the early 1980's was in Coral Springs, Florida, at a bar called Danny's, owned by Danny Chichester.

I have a lot of stories about both establishments.

I should probably start by telling about how I started tending bar in the first place.

I moved from Vermont to Columbia, Maryland in September, 1979, with my wife Wendy.

After leaving the funeral business and moving to Maryland, it was hard for me to find a job. I ended up waiting on tables at Clyde's restaurant. After starting there we had our first child, R.T.

Wendy didn't want to work anymore. My answer was, "If we are going to struggle on one income, we aren't going to do it in Maryland. We are moving to Florida."

My brother Jack was living there and my brother Mickey was moving there in September too.

Jack's wife, my sister-in-law Kathy, got me the job at Harpers in Stuart, Florida.

She was working in the real estate business for one of the partners (Charlie), and put the squeeze on Charlie to get me the job.

Al, the manager at Harpers, wasn't too keen on hiring me, but had no choice. Al, fearing I didn't have any bartending experience, sent me to bartender school in West Palm Beach.

Al had hired all female bartenders and cocktail servers. I was the only male. The staff wore body suits with sarongs, obviously showing off the female physique.

I wore a shirt and tie.

Grand opening night, I show up fresh from bartender school, ready to start my first bartending shift at 4 p.m. Harpers had a big rectangle bar with no opening, so you had to bend down and sneak under to get behind the bar.

So here I am, ready to begin my new profession, with all I had learned at school!

Under the bar I go, and in my excitement I pop up early and scrape my back on the bar top. Feeling some pain, I am going to be a professional and start my career.

Turning to my right, I see my first customer, a huge man, almost twice my size, with an empty bottle of Bud in front of him.

Here we go.

"Sir, can I get you another bottle of Bud?"

The man looks at me and says, "Where are your tits?"

"Sir, I don't have tits."

The man, "Well then, I will wait for the girl who has the tits!"

"Thank you sir."

That is how I started my career in the "hospitality business".

Harper's was a great place to start my career. I had a good time there and left with some great stories. Here are a few:

IT'S A SUNDAY NIGHT AND I'm working by myself. I have my back to the front door, but I can hear some customers coming in. When I have a chance to turn around, there are four red necks sitting at my bar.

I never try to pre-judge, but I don't have a good feeling about these four.

They ask for four Buds and I get them, against my best judgement.

A few minutes later, they are getting a little rowdy, and then I notice that none of them have shoes on. Looking out the door, I see a big four wheeler. Well, these boys have been out all day four wheeling and drinking and are getting ready to start problems in the bar.

I approach them, knowing I am by myself and no match, four to one.

I am a lover not a fighter -- maybe a shitty lover, but a far worse fighter.

"Boys," I say, "You have to move on."

I see their feathers getting ruffled, I explain to them that they can't stay because they are shoeless, but if they leave without a problem, their beers are on me.

Well, this makes them happy. They down their beers and head out the door and head to the next bar. The next day, I hear about the red necks going to another bar and not being let in because of their bare feet.

They got in their four wheeling machine and drove the vehicle through the front door.

The red neck driver told the police he thought he had it in reverse. Yah, sure!

One night, I'm tending bar, when I hear the unmistakable sound of someone throwing up.

I go down the bar and there is this drunk who just threw up on the bar.

Harpers has a tile bar top with grout lines, and I know this isn't going to be fun cleaning up!

I grab a couple of bar mops and start wiping up the bar, as this drunk sits there and doesn't say a word. He just stares at me. When I am just about done cleaning up the mess, he speaks up, asking, "Hey, can I have another drink?"

I look at him and say, "You just puked on my bar, I had to clean up this mess, and you want another drink?"

He says, "Yeah, my mouth tastes like shit and I want to get the taste out."

I look at him for a second, and think about what he just said. I know he is right. I am sure his mouth tastes like shit!

Ah, the hell with it. I give him another drink!

Story #3

MY CHEMISTRY TEACHER

My major in college at Hudson Valley Community College was Mortuary Science.

In my senior year we had to take chemistry, not one of my best subjects – if, now that I think about it -- I had any good subjects!

Chemistry class started at 1 p.m., so on our first day we had some time for lunch before class. A couple of us went across the street to "G" building, which was actually The Grove Bar and Grill!

Having a beer and a burger, I look over to the bar and see this guy pounding a couple of beers and shots! Looking more closely, I recognize the guy. He is our chemistry teacher!

So I tell the guys I'm with that. It's our teacher. They tell me, "No way!"

I say, "OK, but I think it is."

We finish up and head to class, leaving the guy at the bar to finish his beer. Sitting in the class waiting for the professor, who comes in, popping certs. He is the guy at the bar! Holy Shit!

We don't say anything but over the next month or so we see him at the bar when we go for lunch and every day he comes to class popping the certs!

Well, we weren't going into the lab until next semester, so this guy always needed an overhead projector to teach class. One day he shows up, popping his certs, and lo and behold there is no overhead projector!

He becomes real flustered, and starts a little ranting and raving! I raise my hand and he looks at me, and asks what I want?

I say, "Professor, since there isn't an overhead projector, maybe we should conduct this class across the street at the Grove! I will be glad to buy the first pitcher!

He looks at me for a second, then says "Why the hell not!"

So we proceed across the street to the Grove, grab a table and he starts teaching class! I went from a C to an A in the class, and this went on for about a month or so!

Then one day he doesn't show up. We hustle our asses out of the Grove and get back across the street to the classroom as fast as we can.

There waiting for us is another professor. Nothing was said, and we asked no questions. But I went from an A in the class back to a C.

Story #4

Amazing What Kids Hear

Sue and I started dating when Kelly was one-year-old.

When we finally moved in together, Kelly was just starting pre-school. Sue worked in the ER, and so she had to go into work early to start her shift. It was up to me to get Kelly to school. I would get her going and dressed, and then we would head off to Dunkin Donuts for a pink donut and milk, every morning.

Not much on the healthy side, but there are worst ways to start your day.

I have what I call a BOB (Bar Owners Belly) and I am always rubbing my belly and saying, "I can't wait till I have this baby"! Or, "I'm not going to have this baby till I find out who the father is, because I don't want to pay for the college education by myself." Or, "I am not going to have the baby naturally. I am going for a C Section."

So I drop off Kelly each morning at Mrs. Dingo's class. After the first month, they have parent/teacher conferences. Sue goes to meet with Mrs. Dingo.

After telling Sue that Kelly is doing fine, she asks Sue if she can speak to her privately. They go into a corner and Mrs. Dingo tells Sue, "Kelly thinks that TJ is pregnant and when he has the baby, she wants the baby in her room!"

Well you can imagine the look on Sue's face!

That night Sue tells me what happened. I think I almost wet my pants laughing! But Sue is not happy.

So the next morning we have to explain to Kelly that I am not pregnant, and that there is no baby!

After some tears are shed, I think we get her to understand. It's amazing what kids pick up!

Here is another example of what kids hear, again with Kelly.

At Carmody's, I had our own root beer with our label on it. Funny enough, the company that's makes the root beer is owned by a Carmody, no relation though.

I have a great story about the Carmody clan -- will get that later.

Anyway, when we are busy at the restaurant, I always go up to the tables to make sure everything is all right. Sometimes the customers will comment on the root beer, and I tell them my mother makes it in the cellar.

Then, I stomp my foot on the floor and yell down, "Hey Mom, we need another."

This usually gets a chuckle out of the table.

One night Sue and I are having dinner with the kids and Kelly pipes up, saying, "Can we go into the cellar to see TJ's Mom?"

Now I have to explain to Kelly that my mom lives in Florida and someone else makes the root beer!

It is amazing what kids hear!

The Carmody Clan

About the Carmody Clan –

When we are in Ireland with my brothers, we were going through these towns and I was seeing Murphy's Pub, O'Connell's Pub, Dermody's Pub, etc., but no Carmody's Pubs!

Well I ask our bus driver "Is there any Carmody's Pub out there?"

He tells us there is a little town called Listol, where there is a bunch of Carmody's. The next morning before we head to the golf course, he drives us to Listol.

There we see a Carmody's Pub, and a Carmody's Liquor Store! The name is all over the place! Well, after golf, we shower and head to Listol!

Our first stop is Carmody's Pub. Twelve us of walk in, I don't think there has been that many people in that pub at one time ever before!

The barmaid was overwhelmed, till we told her we were a bunch of Carmody's. She told us that her husband was Michael Carmody, and that he was the owner. My brother Michael introduced himself to her. And after a couple of pints, we find out Michael's brother Jack owns the liquor store up the street, so then my brother Jack and I walk up to the store and go in.

Well, the liquor store is in the guy's living room, with a curtain separating the store from the rest of the house!

My brother Jack asks if Jack Carmody is in. The lady behind the counter says "Who be askin'?"

Jack says, "Jack Carmody!"

Next thing you know this guy comes out from behind the curtain and says he is Jack Carmody.

Well, it's old home week then, with everyone hugging everyone else. My brother Jack says that the rest of the family is down at the pub, and asks if Irish Jack would like to join us for a pint!

Irish Jack says, "Yes I would," and starts to put his jacket on.

All of a sudden his wife reaches over, grabs has jacket and says, "No you won't!"

Jack and I look at each other and get out of there as fast as we can before the fight starts!

Back at the pub, after about four rounds, we decide it is time for some dinner. The pub doesn't serve food, so they send us to a restaurant.

The word is out in Listol that there is a bunch of Carmody's in town from the states. Everyone with the name Carmody stops by to see us. I get talking to a

Vincent Carmody. He is the Post Master. (Where does an Irish guy get the name Vincent??)

So I ask Vincent how he is related to Jack and Michael, who own the liquor store and pub. This is what Vincent says to me:

"Yank! I am going to explain it to you in a way that a Yank will understand! It's like the states. You have the Sioux and the Cherokees. They are Indians, but from different tribes. Here in Ireland there are a bunch of Carmody's, but we are from different clans."

I think I had enough to drink by then to actually be able to understand what he was talking about!

Story #6

CROSS YOUR LEGS!

I have two boys from my first marriage. These are stories about their births.

R.T. -- We lived in Columbia, Maryland, when R.T. was born. Wendy goes into labor one night, not waking me up until it is really, really time to go to the hospital for the delivery.

I have the company car, and we head out early Sunday morning. I grab a black garbage bag and put it on the cloth passenger seat, just in case her water breaks. I drive like a maniac to the hospital, pull in, park the car, and go to the nurses' station.

I can tell Wendy is ready.

The nurses tell us we need to fill out paper work first. While we stand there, Wendy's water breaks.

To hell with the paper work!

We jump to the head of the line ahead of about six couples who have been waiting for hours for something to happen. Sorry!

[32]

So not long thereafter, R.T. makes his grand entrance.

I was a very proud father, but it was March 15th, two days before St. Patrick's Day. Perhaps Wendy could have crossed her legs and held on for two more days, but she and R.T. knew it was for the better because I would probably have been in the delivery room with a green beer if it was the 17th!

PATRICK: We had moved to Florida when Wendy became pregnant with Patrick. I tended bar, and we had no health insurance. We were cash customers at the doctor's office and at the hospital. We made weekly payments to both to pay our bills.

So it's a Saturday night in November and we are at home. I'm watching one of my favorite movies, "Blazing Saddles."

Wendy starts having labor pains around 9:30, and around 10:30 we decide to go to the hospital. I call my mother to come and babysit RT. We get to the hospital and are checking in at the nurses' station, when the nurse notices that we are cash customers. She tells us that she is going to put us into a side room, and if we can hang in there until midnight, she will check us in then. That way, we will check in on Sunday and will leave on Monday, and only get charged for Sunday.

Off we go, with me gallantly telling Wendy to cross her legs. We do our Lamaze breathing. Minutes feel like days. The contractions get stronger, but we hang in there. My sister Kathy shows up to give us moral support.

[33]

Breathe. Check the clock. Breathe. Check the clock ... again and again.

The nurse comes in and tells us we can check in now. Wendy says we don't have time to check in. Patrick is ready to see the world. They rush us to the delivery room!

The Doctor rushes in and Patrick arrives at 12:15 a.m., on November 24, 1982.

I don't know how Wendy did it, but I know I was about to hyperventilate with my legs UNCROSSED.

The moral of the story: Get health insurance.

Story #7

SUPER BOWL GAME

In the fall of 1969 I became a Miami Dolphins fan.

I didn't watch a lot of football back then, but it seemed as if everyone else had a team they were cheering for. So I picked the Dolphins. It must have been their uniforms, because I didn't know anything about the team. I am not even sure if I knew where Miami was.

Well, in the fall of 1972 the Dolphins start the beginning of the "Perfect Season".

So the Dolphins make it to the Super Bowl, to be held on Jan. 14, 1973. It's my senior year in high school. A bunch of us decide to rent a motel room in Rutland, Vermont to watch the game.

I am only 17, but we have a couple of guys that are of legal age going up with us. The legal age to buy alcoholic beverages in Vermont then was 18, so getting beer was no problem. I am not sure who rented the room, but the motel we were staying at had an indoor pool, so we were smart enough to bring bathing suits in case we want to take a dip.

Here's how it went:

We arrive in the room. There are about six of us. We get the beer iced down and put the party snacks out. Game time is just before 4 p.m. We check in around 1 p.m., and so by kick off time I feel no pain. The Dolphins are up 14 to 0 at the half.

We all decide to go for a swim. The pool is close to Route 7, so anyone driving by or walking by can look into the pool area and see what's going on. Everything is going fine until the other idiots think it might be funny to attack me and strip me of my bathing suit. I fight like hell, but with five against one, I loose.

Luckily, there is no one else in the pool area, so I jump back in so no one can see me.

I plead for my suit and tell the guys, "Fun is fun. Now give back my bathing suit!"

They decide to go back to the room and leave me there, au naturel.

So there I am in the pool totally naked and trying to figure out my next move.

I look around and see a sauna room in the corner. Ah! Maybe there's a towel or something in there to cover me up. I crawl out of the pool and do that walk everyone does when they are nude in a public place while trying to cover their privates. I scamper into the sauna, and being a lucky guy, there's a towel. What a relief! I head up to the room by the stairs because I don't want to get into a conversation with anybody in the elevator.

I get to the room and bang on the door.

I can hear those assholes laughing like hell. Bang again! Finally, as I am looking over my shoulder to make sure no one is around, the door opens, and before I can react, a hand grabs the towel off me and the door closes. Shit!

There I stand, naked again. Just as I cover up my privates, the door to the room right next to us opens and a family of four walks out. I look at them and they look at me. Those five seconds feel like five hours. Off they go without a word. I bang on the door again with my free hand, and the assholes finally let me in.

They are laughing so hard that they are crying.

I tell them I met our neighbors, and there will probably be some repercussions.

About five minutes later there's a knock on the door, and there stands one of the front desk clerks. He informs us that he has received a complaint about a naked man in the hall. I can't remember who answered the door, but he stays calm, cool, and collected, and tells the clerk that we had seen the same thing and we were just about to come down to complain.

The clerk probably knows what's going on, but doesn't want to get involved, so he tells us if there are any more complaints, the police will be called, and off he goes.

After a few more laughs we settle down to watch the second half. After the Dolphins win, we decide to go out and celebrate at some bar.

Seventeen-years-old and school the next day? Not the smartest decision.

We hit the bar for an hour or so and decide it is time to head back to Manchester, Vermont. Across the street from the bar are railroad tracks with a train moving along slowly. Well, Billy and I decide we are going to take the train back to Manchester and leave the other guys standing there. We run and jump on the train and ride it about a hundred yards.

It stops.

We aren't going to get back to Manchester this way, so we walk back to the bar. The other guys have left, and now we have no ride.

We hoof it through Rutland and make it to Route 7, the road to Manchester. As Billy and I walk along hitch hiking, with hardly any traffic, we come upon the old State Police Barracks. My mistake is to tell Billy what the building was. He grabs a rock and throws it at one of the windows. Crash! We look around and don't see anyone, so we run a little further down the road. A minute later, we hear a car coming, so we put up our thumbs.

Holy shit! The car stops, and the driver asks where we are going. We tell him Manchester, and he tells us to hop in. Off we go for about five miles, when he tells us to get the hell out of his car.

We're in no man's land! No street lights, in the middle of nowhere, past midnight.

What to do, except to keep on walking? About fifteen minutes later, we hear another car. We turn, put out our thumbs, and the car flies by -- I mean really flies by! All of sudden, we see brake lights, and then back up lights. Awesome, we've got a ride. As the car gets closer we see lights on top of it.

It's a State Police cruiser.

Oh yeah, we get a ride right to the NEW State Police barracks.

They split us up for questioning. Billy denies everything. I, with my altar boy guilt, tell them everything. They finally let us call our parents. My father leaves Manchester immediately to pick me up, none too happy though. Billy's parents won't come and get him.

Waiting for my father is like waiting for the electric chair.

When he gets there, he is not a happy camper. He nearly loses it when I ask him if we could give Billy a ride home.

It's a long, very long thirty mile ride home. We drop Billy off. My father reads me the riot act and I lose use of the family car for a while. A couple of months later we go for a court hearing. My father drives, and I listen to how stupid I was. We get there, and Billy is with his mother. The four of us wait for the judge to call us up. The time comes, and the officer doesn't show up, so they drop the case.

Dodged a bullet!

But I still have to listen to my father all the way back to Manchester, another long -- very long -- thirty mile ride home.

That season the Miami Dolphins won every game and my court record remained unblemished.

Story #8

T.J.'S BAR & HIBATCHI

I graduated from High School in 1973 and went immediately to work for E.P. Mahar and Son Funeral Home in Bennington, Vermont.

I commuted from Manchester for the first few months, but decided it was time to get my own apartment. At the ripe old age of 17, I rented my first apartment.

So at the time, I am the only young guy in Bennington with his own apartment, so it soon becomes party central.

Of course the apartment is the size of a shoe box with a small bedroom, even smaller living room, kitchen and bathroom. But we find room to party. We play cards on a directional sign we borrowed from the state, balanced on our knees.

If anyone has to go to the bathroom, we stop the game.

I am working at the Funeral Home full time and everyone else is going to school or is unemployed. After a night of partying, I get up at 7:30 a.m. to go to work and there are bodies sleeping on my couch, chairs and floor. Stepping over them I head to work.

I come home for lunch and they are all still there, watching Star Trek.

At that point, I decide to get a roommate and rent a bigger place. So, in the spring of 1975, I move to an apartment above the Downstairs Attic Antique store. And that's where I decide to build my first bar: T.J.'s Bar and Hibachi.

We "borrow" some barn board from one of my friend's father's old barn for the front of the bar and use the directional sign for the top. It's pretty cool looking.

I get paid on Fridays, about $75.00 a week, with $60.00 to take home.

I call all my friends and let them know that the bar will be open Friday night.

The legal drinking age in Vermont at the time is 18, so I'm legal. I go to the liquor store and spend the whole sixty on booze, beer, mixers, ice and cups. At 7 p.m. the bar is open and I am the bartender. Fifty cents a drink, beer or booze, except for one – a $2.50 drink we call Daffy Ducks Nuts, served in a Looney Tune glass from McDonalds.

Just fill the glass with Black Velvet Whiskey to the bottom of Daffy's nuts, and drink it as a shot. I think there are only about four of us who do the shot. We have to carry one or two down the stairs to get them home.

I keep track of the money, and as soon as I get my sixty bucks back, it's open bar!

(This was my first mistake in the bar business. I should have kept charging to make a profit, but I was having too much fun).

So the party goes on, and the next morning I head off to work at the funeral home, stepping over bodies on the floor. I come back at noon and as usual they are watching TV and raiding the fridge.

After Friday night there was always booze left over, stuff like gin that nobody would drink the night before, so we would open up the bar again for free and drink the rest of the booze. On Sunday morning, I might have to go into the Funeral Home, once again stepping over bodies.

On one of these Saturday night parties, a couple of girls think it would be funny to stick a can of Very Berry Hawaiian Punch in the oven of my kitchen range. On Sunday morning, I have to prepare the Funeral Home for calling hours from 2 p.m. to 4 p.m., and 7p.m. to 9 p.m.

In between the calling hours I go home to try to get a nap, get something to eat, and then go back to work.

This Sunday, I come home to have a burger and fries before I go back to work. I turn the oven on to warm it up to bake fries rather than fry them. I take off my suit and hang it up in the kitchen. I immediately fall asleep on the couch. After about 45 minutes, the two girls knock on my door for a visit. We are in the living room talking, when all of a sudden we hear a big bang!

The stove door blows off and flies across the kitchen. Very Berry Hawaiian Punch is sizzling all over the walls, ceiling and on my suit!

I look at these girls and ask what the fuck happened, and they say they put the can in the stove as a joke. Some joke! If I had been putting my fries in the oven at the time Very Berry Hawaiian punched out, I could have lost my head. Needless to say, I go back to the funeral home smelling very berry!

But I must also say, I had some great times at my first bar the summer President Nixon resigned!

Story #9

HANGING THE MOON!

It's a Sunday night in Coral Springs, Florida, and I'm tending bar at Danny's.

Sundays are crazy. We have a DJ, and he plays to a younger crowd who can afford to be out drinking on a Sunday. We make it to last call and we're at the bar having a drink -- me, Tony the doorman, and Kim, one of the waitresses.

Kim asks if we have heard about the new strip bar just south of Sample Road on US 1. She tells us that on one side they have female strippers and on the other they have male strippers. The strip club stays open till 4:00 a.m. and it's only about 2:30 p.m. on a Sunday night.

Would we like to go there have a drink?

Tony and I look at each other and say, "Why not?"

Off we go in Tony's big four door Italian Chevy ... something. Tony drives, Kim sits in the middle and I ride shotgun.

We make it to the club in time to go in for a couple of cocktails, Kim heads to the male stripper side and Tony and I to the other. We agree to meet up at last call. After a few drinks, we hook up with Kim and head back home on

Sample Road with the same seating arrangements in Tony's car.

We are driving along, and a car darts out from a side street and cuts us off. Tony slams on the brakes, and we all swear at the driver. I tell Tony to pull up right next to the asshole at the next light so I can give him the full moon. Tony is okay with that, so we ease up next to the car at the next light. I put down the window, jump up on to the seat, drop my pants, stick my shiny white ass out the window, and laugh like hell, until I hear Kim scream, "He has a gun!"

I look over my shoulder and there's a gun pointed at my ass!

Kim, screaming, ducks to the floor. I'm screaming too, and I jump on top of her!

Tony, also screaming, hits the gas! Now, the guy is chasing us. Lucky for us, Tony is able to outrun the guy, and he gives up on us.

The rest way home we are laughing like crazy, knowing we dodged a bullet ... literally! I'm also thinking of how I could explain to my wife why the hell I have a bullet in my ass ... but no hole in my pants!

THE ROCK STAR

Ever since I was a little kid, St. Patrick's Day has been my favorite day. And, I have owned pubs and restaurants, which has given me plenty of opportunities to plan my own parties.

The last of my bar years, when I owned Carmody's in downtown Bennington, Vermont, we started St. Patrick's Day at 10 a.m.

Here's how it went:

The bag piper meets me at one of the nursing homes in Bennington. I'm dressed in my leprechaun outfit and I have a couple hundred green carnations.

We go into the home. He plays and I hand out the carnations. Most of the residents are very appreciative, but some of them put their hands over their ears and some of them throw the carnations back at me.

We usually stop at four nursing homes. The last one is the Old Soldiers Home.

My bag piper plays the Marine Hymn, and you get a tear in your eye watching the residents straighten up and salute when they hear it.

After our last stop, we head to the bar. That's around noon. The place is buzzing. The band is setting up for a 1 p.m. start. The bar starts to fill up with the hardy ones ready to start the festivities early with hopes they will last until the end.

I have the piper start off with a couple of songs to get everyone in the spirit. Lunch time is busy. Everyone comes for the corned beef sandwiches and the corned beef dinner. Around 1 p.m. the band starts and my day really starts. I begin with a green beer, knowing I have to pace myself until I give last call around midnight.

Starting at 2 p.m. and every hour after that, I get on the bar and sing three songs: *Seven Old Ladies Stuck in a Lavatory, Green Alligators,* and *Wild Irish Rover.* The band plays the songs and I get the crowd going.

Early in the day, the smaller crowd sings along with me. Around 8 p.m., I get on the bar and have my "Rock Star" experience.

The bar is packed. As soon as I get on the bar the place goes crazy. I love it. A couple hundred people are there. I can only imagine what it's like to do a concert in a stadium. I repeat the gig at 9 p.m., 10 p.m., and 11 p.m.

Around midnight, I go up for the last time with the crowd all liquored up. They are ready ... and so am I.

I do the three Irish songs and I finish up with Piano Man and American Pie. They are screaming and going wild. I jump off the bar and go hide. The bartenders come from behind the bar. No more cocktails! I've made enough money by then, and it's time to send everyone home.

Some St. Patrick Day Highlights:

The Piper and I are at one of the nursing homes. We are in the lunch room. He is playing and I am handing out carnations and Carmody's root beer. One of the nurses asks the residents what they think the piper has under his kilt.

One resident, a 90-year-old partially blind woman in a wheel chair, answers, "I am not sure what he has under his kilt, but if you bring him over here I'll find out!"

One year, I didn't have a bagpiper for St. Patrick's Day. It was around 2 p.m. in the afternoon, and I was having my first green beer, drowning my sorrow at the thought of going through a whole St. Pat's Day without a piper.

All of a sudden, one of the waitresses comes up to me and says there is a guy playing the pipes outside the restaurant. I tell her, "Don't joke with me. I'm not happy about the situation."

She says she's not joking. "There really is a guy playing the pipes outside."

I jump off my bar stool and head outside. Standing there is a piper in his whole regalia! Holy Shit! A miracle! So I ask him, "What the hell is going on?"

He replies that he has recently moved to town, has no place to play, knows that I have a regular piper, but was wondering if it would be okay to play in front of the restaurant.

My answer is, "Get your butt inside! Here is the deal: You are going to get paid. Your beer and food are free. You play when I tell you and until I tell you it's time to go."

That's when I met Merrick, my new Piper.

Merrick makes my day. He's awesome! Around 11 p.m. he comes up to me and asks if it's okay to go home.

I tell him, "Off with you my man. This is the beginning of a great relationship!"

LIFE'S NOTHINGBUT A PARADE

My mother always told us we were Irish. It took years to finally make if official, though, when a cousin showed up at Carmody's bar with a copy of the family tree (but that's another story!).

When we were kids and St. Patrick's Day rolled around, my mother made sure we would celebrate it by wearing something green to school ... going to Mass ... and by eating corned beef and cabbage for dinner.

No green beer, not yet!

When I got close enough to the legal drinking age (I guess I was 16 at the time), I decided it was my duty to celebrate St. Patrick's Day the old fashioned way – by getting drunk!

Growing up, I never actually went to a St. Patrick's Day parade, but I used to watch the New York City parade on the old WPIX TV station.

The first time I was involved in a real St. Patrick's Day Parade was when I was running Danny's in Coral Springs. Danny was the Grand Marshall, and as it turned out, the parade was a great experience for me. In fact that was the last time I saw a parade that I wasn't either running or involved in, until 2010, when I watched the Holyoke Parade in Holyoke, Massachusetts.

I have started five different St. Patrick Day parades in three different states.

#1. Bennington, Vermont: We had opened PT's Pub, and the first St. Patrick's Day there fell on a Saturday. I decide to run my first St. Pat's parade that day. It wasn't going to be very big, but we were going to have fun.

So I start setting up the parade. I pick out a Grand Marshall, a guy by the name of Dave Brady, who came from a family of about eight, which guaranteed that we'd have people to view the event. I found a piper and a drummer, and put up signs in the bar to spread the word that if anyone wanted to participate, all they had to do was let me know.

The plan was for St Patrick's Day to get started at 8 a.m. with an Irish breakfast, with the parade starting at 11 a.m., followed by Irish entertainment at 1:00 p.m.

Partying was to continue for the rest of the day!

On the Friday night before, the bar is packed and the DJ is rocking the crowd.

All of sudden there are two cops at the front door, asking to speak to me.

I approach them and recognize both of them right away. I ask them, "What's going on?"

They ask me if I am running a parade tomorrow. I reply that I am. Then they ask me if I have a permit.

"Shit no! Do I need one?"

They answer, "Yes!"

And thinking fast on my feet, I ask them if I need a permit to run a funeral procession. They look at each other and tell me I don't need a permit for a funeral procession, but I can't have any marchers. Everyone needs to be in a vehicle, and all traffic lights and signs must be obeyed.

"Of course!"

I thank them and tell them that we will – in fact -- be having a funeral procession the next day, and they reply that's okay, but they will be watching ... and will of course arrest anyone breaking the law.

"Shit! Now what do I do?"

Well, that night at the bar and the next morning I round up everyone I know who has any kind of truck ...

St. Patrick's Day starts out great. Breakfast is going good and we have a nice crowd. Around 10:30 I start organizing the parade. I have about ten trucks lined up and a 1940 Buick convertible for the Grand Marshall.

Okay, so at 10:55 a.m., everyone is outside. The bar is closed! I line up everyone. The Grand Marshall is in the Buick; the piper, the drummer and I, we're all in the next truck. Brady's family is in the next truck, and the rest of the patrons in other trucks.

Off we go! We make a right on to North Street with our funeral procession, and as we make the corner, and in front of the old A&P store are people sitting in their lawn chairs waiting for this thirty second parade!

We drive by, and everyone is cheering! What a great feeling! Off we go to Main and North, where we have to make a left hand turn to go up Main. The light turns red and the procession is waiting. I look around to see if there are any cops around. None!

The light changes and we start making the turn, and again there are people waiting for my thirty second parade! All the trucks make the light, and up Main we go toward a small but cheering crowd.

Then we make a U-turn at Safford Street and head back down Main to the same small, but cheering crowd.

After hitting every single red light, the funeral procession makes it back to the bar! Not one cop in sight. We go inside and have a grand celebration!

#2. Stuart Florida: I am a partner in a restaurant called Sharkey's Tropical Grill on US 1 in Stuart. I decide I want to run a small St. Patrick's Day Parade in Downtown Stuart. Learning from the first one, I know that I need a permit. I approach City Hall and get everything done right. At the same time, I ask the mayor to participate in the parade. I tell him I'd like him to paint the green stripe down the street to lead the parade. He tells me, "It would be an honor!"

Parade day comes. We have a nice line up, a bagpiper group, some civic groups, school kids, and a couple of other floats. It's a beautiful day and everyone is in a festive mood. I'm ready to start the parade and can't find the mayor! After asking everyone if they have seen the mayor, a big black guy approaches me. I ask him if I can help him, and he replies that he is the vice- mayor. The mayor had to go out of town and he is here to lead the parade by painting the green stripe down the street!

"Holy Shit! My first real St. Patrick's Day parade and I have a black man here to lead the parade?

"Let's do this!"

Well, the vice-mayor leads the parade and really gets into it! He's dancing down the street while painting the stripe. Everyone is following him! The parade is a great success! I can't thank him enough.

#3. T.J. O'Carmody's in Hoosick Falls, New York. This was the start of a parade that is still going on to this day.

I start by picking out my Grand Marshall -- Mike Conway.

Mike used to own a bar in Hoosick Falls and was well known as the Irish guy in town. So Mike and I go together to the town offices to get the permits. He also takes me to Troy, New York, to meet four bar owners who had a connection to another guy from Hoosick Falls by the name of Rock Murphy. He was from Hoosick Falls but had a bar in Troy. Rock passed away and these bar owners used to run a memorial golf tournament in Hoosick Falls -- in honor of Rock.

The bar owners are all in, and say they will bring a crew to the parade.

Now we have to work on the rest of the floats.

Hoosick Falls has a good Irish contingency, and a lot of folks are willing to participate, along with most of the bars in Hoosick Falls and a couple of bars in Bennington.

The parade is starting to get big!

Parade day comes and it is sunny, but freezing. Oh well, the show must go on.

This is going to be my best parade yet! Bands, floats, politicians and the Grand Marshall.

I start the parade in the empty lot across from the bar with the Grand Marshall first, sending his car on its way towards the downtown area. I organize the bands and the rest of the floats. One is a hot tub on wheels.

Now, every float is gone, except mine. I hop on it, and off we go, turning the corner, and to my surprise there are two to three thousand people out waiting for the parade!

The hair on the back of my neck is standing up! Awesome!

The rest of the day goes great, with people pub crawling in Hoosick Falls all day, bouncing around and having a great time! My first real St. Patrick's Day parade in Hoosick Falls is a great success!

#4. I closed down the bar in Hoosick and went to Myrtle Beach for a while, and then came back to Bennington to open T.J.'s and Mike's in North Bennington.

I decide I want to have another parade. The only problem is that North Bennington and Hoosick Falls NY are only about 8 miles apart and I don't want to compete with the parade I started over there 3 years ago.

So I meet with Kevin and Marie, who are running the parade, and work out a deal. They will run their parade on Saturday, which is a good day for them and the other bars in Hoosick Falls, and I will run my parade on Sunday. That will give me an extra money making day that weekend after a busy Friday and Saturday.

A St Patrick's Day weekend for bars is like Black Friday for retailers.

I go about planning the parade, pick the Grand Marshall, Eddie P----, and get the permission for the parade from the town. The Parade in Hoosick Falls is big and they come back out on Sunday for my parade. Both are a success!

Some St. Patrick's Day parade highlights:

1. The second parade in Hoosick Falls was during a blizzard in March, 1990.

The police are telling me not to run the parade because the streets are bad and the wind is howling. Being a stubborn Irishman, I run the parade anyway. A snow plow leads the police, the bagpiper, the Grand Marshall, a float from the Polish Hall, one from the Steak House in Bennington, and my float with the Seven Old Ladies.

The parade starts. The weather is awful and we are making our way through town. I run up to the police officer in charge and tell him to cut it short and take us back to the bar! Why? Because I thought I was crazy for running the parade, but not as crazy as the people sitting on the snow banks with their beers waiting for the parade to come by.

2. One Armed Grand Marshall: The Grand Marshall one year was a bartender, Tommy Ryan. Tommy had a stroke a few years earlier, and the use of his left side was limited, but he was able to still tend bar at the Country Club. Not the fastest, but you always got your drink.

Parade day is here, and I have Tommy waiting at the bar until I get ready to start the parade. I don't want him to be standing in the March chill. I have everyone lined up and I send a golf cart to bring Tommy up so we can start the parade.

I own a limousine with a sun roof and that is what I am going to have Tommy ride in because he can't walk well. Tommy arrives and I try to get him into the limo. Getting a one-armed, one-legged man through the sunroof of a limousine is not easy.

Everyone is waiting, from the priest, to the bagpiper, to the bands and the floats. Here I am looking like a pig trying to screw a football into the back of a limo! Poor Tommy and I are rolling around, when I final tell him to get ready with his good hand because I am grabbing him by his belt and giving one last push to get through the sunroof.

Finally, he is through! But now I have a Grand Marshall, holding on for dear life with his good hand, not able to raise his other hand to wave to the crowd! He survives the parade and says he had a great time. Note to myself, don't try that again!

3. The Good Padre: We had a priest in North Bennington who led the parade for the three years I held it there. He really got into the day. One year we bought him green vestments to wear for the parade. That year he shows up to lead the parade and you would have thought it was St. Patrick himself. (I think a little bit of the holy wine gave him some liquor courage).

The Padre followed the bagpiper in all his glory, waving, giving blessings, shaking hands. It was probably as close to being the Pope he would ever get!

4. Seven Old Ladies: My float for the St. Patrick's Parade has always been the Seven Old Ladies, which is based on an Irish song about seven old ladies getting stuck in the lavatory. It's a crazy song that I would sing atop the bar every St. Patrick's Day.

Every year it was an honor for a man or a woman to be chosen as one of the seven old ladies. They would dress in somewhat outlandish feminine garb, get on a float with a boom box playing the song, and sing along very loudly, nearly in tune.

We were always the last float, and we would get the loudest cheers! To the old ladies over the years, I hope you are unstuck for a rousing "Thank You!"

Story #12

STUDENT COUNCIL PRESIDENT

In my junior year of high school, my sister Patty was a senior. My only goals in school were to play sports, date as many girls as possible, and set up a lot of parties.

And I was pretty good at all three!

Like this: My sister Patty comes up with a great idea! She thinks I should run for student council vice president.

I ask her, "Why I would want to do that?"

She says it would look good on my transcripts.

My question is, "What the hell is a transcript?"

I guess I'm not thinking about college at the time. My sister suggests that as vice president, I don't really have to do anything except show up at the meetings.

I'm thinking, "I guess I can handle that."

So I run for vice president at the end of my junior year, and my campaign is successful!

The beginning of my senior year, the Student Council meetings start and as my sister suggested, I just show up at the meetings and do nothing. All goes well until everyone figures out that the class president is an idiot!

And now, for the first time in all the years that Burr and Burton Seminary has been in existence, it has its first student government impeachment!

Goodbye Mr. President. Hello Mr. Vice President ... you are now Mr. President.

For a guy who can't spell 'parliamenterry proceedure', I think I do a pretty good job.

I open a smoking room for the students, we do some fund raisers, and we were always the first in-line at the cafeteria for lunch on the days of the council meetings.

As my senior year progresses with soccer, basketball, golf and a few other extracurricular activities, spring is quickly upon us. At BBS, it is a school policy that we get out of school on Fridays at 1 p.m. So basically we have half a day off. I come up with a great idea, one that will help the classes bond together, and also develop some friendly competition.

I approach the school's headmaster with my idea.

I want to have a field day on one of the last Fridays before the school year ends. We will have all the classes compete against each other in soccer, field hockey and softball. And the winning class gets a trophy until the next year.

So, the Headmaster thinks this is a great idea, and tells me to set it up, so I'm off and running.

At the same time, one of my best friends and co-party planners, Greg, decides it would be a great idea to set up a little pre-field day party -- a four kegger -- to be held at the Manchester airport at 6 a.m. on the morning of the field day.

Greg and I are busy planning both events, when I find out that the impeached president has notified the police about the little pre-party we have planned.

Now I am not one to cancel a party, so we make an alternative plan. We move the party to a field in Dorset, Vermont, and tell all the potential participants about change in plans -- everyone *except for the past president.*

On the day of the party, at 6 a.m., the police raid the airport and no one is there!

But in a field in Dorset, on a beautiful sunny spring morning, there are about 100 party animals enjoying a pre-field day party. There are no ID's checked, and we have kids from all the classes there, some having their first beer! The music is blaring, the beer is flowing, and everyone is having a good time.

As president, I know I have to act responsibly, and give last call at 7:30 a.m., so everyone can get to the field day on time.

And we all show up on campus feeling great and ready for the games to begin.

All of sudden, things go downhill quickly. Kids are puking in the bushes. Some are passed out and everyone stinks of beer. The field day is quickly cancelled, parents are called to pick up their kids, and the beautiful day turns into a cluster fuck.

Now Monday morning arrives, and Greg and I are summoned to the headmaster's office!

This isn't going to be good.

As Greg and I take our seats, I can see the fury in the headmaster's face. The first question out of his mouth is, "What the hell were you two thinking?"

Our answer was that we guessed we weren't really thinking. Probably not the best answer. But what the hell, we are going down anyway.

His next question is, "What am I going to do with the two of you?"

My answer to this question is either going to save us or really put us into the shitter!

I reply that since that the school year is almost over and we both will be graduating and out of there soon, I say that it wouldn't do any good to throw us out at that point.

I think he is a little shocked at the answer, but he thinks about it for a minute.

He replies that if we do anything wrong, even if we fart wrong, we never will graduate, and will probably be there for the rest of our lives. Then, we are excused from the office and get through the last few days without screwing up again.

We do have plans for a graduation party ... but that's another story.

Story #14

THE ALTAR

I went to a Catholic grammar school for eight years --
which probably explains why I have this nervous twitch.
(Gotta love those nuns!).

In the sixth grade, you were expected to become an
altar boy. I did with great pride, learning Latin for the first
time, or more truthfully, learning how to mumble Latin,
since I could never learn it. Then the Church decided to do
the Mass in English, so I did the same thing I did with the
Latin. I learned how to mumble the words enough to get
by.

In the eighth grade I became one of the head altar
boys, which meant I could go to funerals. That meant I got
out of class to do them! I also could attend weddings,
which meant I could get tipped by the best man. I have two
stories: One is about a wedding and one is about a
funeral.

The Wedding: It's a spring day on a Saturday
morning, and the wedding is scheduled for 11 a.m. I walk
to the church at around 10 to get everything ready for the
Mass. The wine needs to get poured into the claret jugs
(Always take a sip, just to make sure it hasn't gone sour.

You don't want the priest to get bad wine. Ah ... just one more sip just to make sure). The candles have to be lit, and you have to get dressed in your cassock.

There's plenty to do.

Around 10:30 a.m. the best man and the groomsmen show up at the back of the church. The guests start to arrive. The priest shows up, and starts to get himself ready for the service. You can feel the excitement in the air as the 11th hour approaches.

The bride shows up in her limo and she's waiting to enter the church. All the guests are seated. The priest and the altar boys are ready, and so are the groomsmen and the bridesmaids.

Only one small problem. No Groom!

Well, everyone in the church is abuzz. This is long before cell phones, so people are running around trying to figure out where the groom is. He's nowhere to be found!

So everyone leaves the church in shock. The priest and the altar boys head to the back of the church to put everything away, blow out the candles, and pour the wine back (Just one more sip to make sure the wine hasn't gone bad).

I walk back home and my sister asks about the wedding. I tell her the groom didn't show, and she doesn't believe me. I tell her, "You think that's bad? It's worse. I didn't get a tip!"

Thirty years later, I own a restaurant in Bennington, Vermont, and up the street, two brothers own a hot dog stand. I find out one of the brothers is the "groom" who didn't show up for the wedding.

Turns out, he took off for Florida right after the rehearsal dinner!

I always wanted to go up to him and ask for the tip I never got, but I figured if you are running a hot dog stand, you probably need the five bucks more than I do!

The Funeral: We used to get out of school to serve funeral masses. Most of the funerals were at 10 a.m. That meant we could get out of school at 9:30 to go to the church and get everything ready: Light the candles, light the incense, get our cassocks on, and taste the wine to make sure it's okay. Maybe taste it a second time.

This particular funeral Mass starts, as all of them did, when the funeral directors get the casket into the back of the church and then get the family lined up.

One of the funeral directors hits a buzzer to sound in the sacristy to let us know they are ready for us. We go out in a procession. I'm carrying the crucifix with the figure of Jesus atop a long staff. Two altar boys are behind me, one with the incense and the other with the holy water. The priest is behind them.

We walk to the back of the church, do the blessing, turn around and head back with the casket and family following us.

The Mass takes about an hour. The priest usually leaves with the funeral directors to go to the cemetery for the final blessing before the burial. That leaves us altar boys to clean up, taste the wine one more time, and then head back to school.

We always stop by the bakery on the way to get doughnuts and arrive at school in time for lunch.

At this particular funeral, we are in the sacristy after Mass, cleaning up and getting ready to take off our cassocks, when the Monsignor tells us to leave our cassocks on because we are going to the cemetery for a graveside ceremony.

What the Monsignor says goes.

So I grab Jesus on the crucifix and staff. One of the other altar boys grabs the holy water and out the church we go. Waiting for us is an Olds 88, with four doors and AC (not many of those around in 1969).

Monsignor hops into the front seat and we altar boys into the back. My brother-in- law Alex is the driver and, one of the funeral directors.

Off we go to Pownal, Vermont, about a thirty minute ride, in a funeral procession. That's OK. The AC feels great!

We pull into the cemetery, and Alex tells us to wait in the car while he gets everything set. After a few minutes, Alex comes and gets us altar boys and tells Monsignor he will be right back for him.

Alex takes the three of us, and places the two other altar boys by the casket. One of them holds the holy water. There is a tent set up over the casket that day because it is so hot. So Alex places me outside the tent at the foot of the casket. I'm holding the Lon g staff with

Jesus on the crucifix. Alex goes back to get the Monsignor. When they get to the grave, the Monsignor tells Alex that he wants the crucifix moved to the other side of the casket towards the sun. Alex comes to get me and we walk between the casket and the family to get to the other side.

Well, there are wooden planks there to keep the grave from collapsing. I'm walking on the planks, when I slip and fall into the grave!

Oh, the gasps from the family and the looks on their faces!

There I am holding on to Jesus, up to my shoulders in the grave under the casket. Alex and Bill Hurley, another funeral director, grab me by my shoulders to pull me out of the grave while I am still holding on to Jesus, I figure if I am going into the grave, he's going with me.

After they get me out of the grave, I am a little shaken and a little bit muddy, but the ceremony must go on. Alex doesn't talk to me for a long while after my fall, and they don't take altar boys to the cemetery after that.

Worst of all, we don't get to get our donuts that day!

THE DRUG TRIAL

After I lose P.T.'s Pub to my partner and move to Florida, an investigation and drug trial begins to move along for my former partner.

I get a subpoena to appear at a deposition in Bennington, Vermont.

My former partner's attorneys want to find out what I know. Well, I'm not going to pay for a flight to Vermont. If they want to hear from me they are going to pay for it. They jerk me around, and I don't get the ticket until the day before I am to fly up there.

I make it to Bennington and get to the deposition, which is being held in a conference room at the courthouse. My brother Jack sets me up with an attorney, just to make sure nothing stupid happens.

I walk into the conference room with my attorney and -- holy shit -- the place is packed!

My former partner's two attorneys, the assistant Attorney General for the State of Vermont, the State Attorney, his assistant, and a couple of detectives are all there. It's standing room only! They do save a couple of seats for me and my attorney. All of them want to hear what I have to say about the drug bust.

I know that my former partner and his attorneys have been telling everyone that the drugs were mine. I live in Florida and I'm unable to defend myself from there, but I'm ready for any questions they're going to ask me in Vermont!

My former partner's lead attorney is this little Jewish attorney from Fort Lauderdale. His expertise is DUI's. He's a good customer of Danny's, because he's gotten quite a few of his customers from Danny's bar.

The very first question in this big drug trial is, "Mr. Carmody, how much coke do you do?"

Well, having been sworn in and under oath, I look this attorney straight in the eye and reply, "I have never done coke in my life. I may have had too many Dewar's and water like you, but I never have done coke!"

You can feel the wind in their defense strategy go out the window. Now, the prosecution is looking at me in a total different light. Maybe he is on our side. I can see that Mr. Dewars' attorney is in shock. He waits a few moments before he asks his next question. "Mr. Carmody, why did your plane ticket cost more than mine?"

What the fuck kind of a question is that? My answer is "You guys booked my flight. I wasn't going to come here without you guys paying for it, so you must not have booked the super saver!"

There are not many more questions, but you can feel the momentum swing to my side. The folks prosecuting my former partner just can't wait to talk to me!

I head back to Florida, forget about the trial, and don't really care what's happening. I'm just glad to clear up my name in this mess. I move back up to Vermont about six months later and hope to open another bar. I tend bar and work at the funeral home part time.

The State Attorney's Office finds out that I'm back in town. They contact me and want to know if I will testify at the drug trial, which is starting in a week.

What the hell! I have the time and I would like to know what's going on.

The trial is in Brattleboro on the other side of the state. I have to be there at 1 p.m. on a Tuesday afternoon. I have just started dating my future wife, Sue. She has Tuesday off, so I ask her if she would like to take a ride over to Brattleboro for lunch, and oh, by the way, we have to stop by for a drug trial after lunch. And she accepts!

Tuesday comes, and Sue and I head over the mountain to Brattleboro. I find us a nice place for lunch. Just as we are getting our lunch, I look up, and who is walking in for lunch? My former partner and his two attorneys!

I slink down so they won't see me, Sue asks, "What's going on?"

I tell her about the new customers. She glances over to check them out. Fortunately, they don't notice us.

We leave the restaurant and head to the courthouse. The courtroom is on the second floor. When I arrive, the state's attorney puts me in a room at the top of the stairs near the courtroom. The door in the room has a little window so you can sneak a peek to see who is in the room, if you want to.

While I am in the room, I hear this car pull up with its muffler in real need of repair. I look out the window and see it's the old limo my former partner and I bought over a year ago. I guess business hasn't been too good because he can't afford to fix the muffler.

Probably all those attorney fees.

While I am in the room, Sue makes herself comfortable in the corridor just outside the court room. We had picked up a couple of newspapers, and she had a book to pass the time. The next thing I know the two detectives in the case and the state's attorney are discussing who the blonde is reading the paper. Is she a secret weapon for the defense? Who is she?

I let them stew on it for a while longer and say, "Hey assholes! She's with me!"

While Sue is sitting there, she observes my former partner and his attorneys make their appearance. Another attorney, not Mr. Dewars, but the Vermont attorney, peeks in the window where I am and sees me.

Sue tells me later, that as soon as he saw me, his whole attitude changed. He runs down the hall, catches up to Mr. Dewars and my former partner, screaming, "Holy Shit! Carmody is here! Holy Shit! Carmody is here!"

Sue says everyone's attitude changed. I guess they didn't think I was going to show and their whole defense hinged on the idea that they were going to pin the drugs on me.

[74]

"Too bad boys. I'm here!"

They don't ask me to testify that day. I go back the next day and sit around again ... when my former partner is found guilty!

Story #16

THE IRISH WAKE

   T.J. O'Carmody's Irish Pub in Hoosick Falls, NY was on a lease, with an option to buy. As we were closing in on the option to buy time, the seller and I didn't see eye to eye, so I decided to walk away from the deal at the end of August.

   Knowing I was going to close down, I decided that I wanted to go out with a bang, so I decided to host my own Irish wake.

   Now having been in the funeral business for years (another chapter in my life) I knew just what to do. Having the contacts in the funeral profession, I was able to get a casket, a kneeler, flower racks, a register stand and book, candles, the whole works. I was going to set this up like a real funeral. I also got a hearse, a limo and a bagpipe player.

   This party was going to be awesome! The only thing I lacked was a body! Well, I was able to take care of that. My future wife, Sue, was a nurse in the ER at the hospital and had a few contacts with the Rescue Squad, so we were able to borrow a "Resuscitation Anne", a doll they used for practicing CPR.

With a little make up, a hat, and some of my clothes, we were able to make Anne look a lot like me.

Now to set up the party: First, no sense doing it on a Saturday night. I am already busy, so let's do it on the last Sunday of the month.

When you are throwing a party, make sure you don't run out of booze, so one call to my Coors distributor, and the next thing I know I have a small trailer available for the party with draft handles on the side, allowing us to serve beer outside.

I don't at that time actually have a license for outside consumption, but who cares? I'm going to turn the license in soon anyway.

Word is out that we are closing. Friday and Saturday are crazy! Sunday comes and now I have to get ready for the Irish Wake. We get the casket set up, put Anne in the casket, apply the makeup, arrange the flowers, the candles, the register stand, and register book. I also have prayer cards made up with the date of the opening of the bar and the closing date.

I know you think this sounds crazy, but some people simply know I am.

I pick out six pallbearers, most of them my bartenders and close friends. Now that everything is set at the bar, it's time for me to get dressed for my own funeral! I dress up in a suit and Sue gets dressed up as the merry widow.

I'm telling you we both look great!

So off to the bar we go. The party starts at 7 p.m. and lots of people start showing up. It's crazy. They go up and kneel down at the casket, come back to Sue and me and tell us how good I look, how sorry they are for our loss.

You had to be there!

Well, around 8:30 p.m. I decide to conduct my own funeral. I take the mike from the DJ. You didn't think I was going to throw a party without some music, did you?

I proceed to thank everyone for their support during the past two years. I thank my staff and I thank the merry widow for putting up with me!

Everyone is into it. I can't believe it! So now I go over and close the casket on myself -- kinda surreal -- and call the pallbearers up to carry the casket out to the waiting hearse.

This is awesome!

The pallbearers hoist the casket onto their shoulders and walk it through the crowd to the hearse, with the bagpiper leading them.

When the casket goes into the hearse, that's supposed to signal the end of the funeral. Everyone is supposed to come back in and party to the wee hours of the morning. But everything is going so smoothly, I decide we should have a funeral procession around town!

I get everybody lined up: Bagpiper first, a 1960's pink Cadillac next, then the hearse, Sue and myself, the pallbearers with the candles, and around 150 other mourners with cocktails in their hands.

Off we go up the side street the bar is on, making a right on to one of the main streets.

This is so crazy!

Trucks are pulling over the let the procession through. People are coming out of their houses to watch the procession, and everyone in the procession is chanting, "TJ! TJ! TJ!"

We go to make a left on one of the side streets so I can bring this procession back to the bar. Then it happens!

A cop car pulls up to the procession. I worry about what the cop is going to do. Everyone steps aside to let the patrol car by so that he can get to me. He slows down, looks at the hearse, shakes his head, pulls around the hearse, gets in front of the bagpiper and leads us back to the bar!

I guess he figures they didn't have enough room in the local jail to lock up 150 people for the night. We get back to the bar and have a great Irish Wake!

Story #17

THE LIMO TRIP

I was working at Danny's in Coral Springs, Florida, when Wendy was pregnant with Patrick. We still lived in Palm City, Florida, and I was commuting back and forth, 80 miles each way. Wendy wanted me to get back to Stuart, so I went down to talk to the folks at Harper's. They hired me back.

My last night at Danny's is a Tuesday night and Danny decides to throw a going away party for me. A ton of people show up. A bunch from Stuart shows up with my brothers Jack and Mickey. The party is great!

Before last call, the boys from Stuart, except for Mickey, head back down the turnpike. Mickey decides to stay and return with me to Stuart the next day because, after last call, we are going back to Danny's house to continue the party. Mickey doesn't want to miss out on any of the fun.

After last call, we head to Danny's and continue partying on until about 3:30 a.m., when everyone decides to call it a night. Mickey and I crash on Danny's couches, and we pass out cold.

We wake up. Everyone is gone: Danny to do his thing, Sandy off to do Real Estate, and the kids off to school. Mickey and I take showers and get dressed in the same clothes we had the night before. It's around 11 a.m. by now, and Mickey says that he is starved and we need to get something to eat before we head back to Stuart.

I come up with the great idea of going back to Danny's, because on Wednesdays, Danny cooks his famous burger on a gas grill in the parking lot.

Wednesday at Danny's is a total fuck-off day. If you want to sneak out of work and have a few cocktails and not be by yourself, you go to Danny's. Everyone knows Danny is going to be there partying. Every beer and liquor salesman in Broward County stops by on Wednesday because they know they will be able to talk to Danny and have a few cocktails themselves!

Mickey and I walk into Danny's around 11:30 a.m., and the place is busy. Almost everyone who was at the party the night before has shown up to have some hair of the dog. Danny's sees us and immediately orders a round of shots. Holy shit! Here we go again! We have a great time. Everyone is partying!

I turn to Mickey around 2 p.m. and tell him we need to get out of here or we'll never make it back to Stuart. He agrees with me. So I go over to Danny and tell him we need to go. He asks me if I can hang in for another half hour. I ask him why, but he just asks us to please wait for a little while. I tell him okay and tell Mickey, so we order another beer.

Within half an hour, a limo shows up. I ask Danny what's going on. He tells me they are going to give me and Mickey a ride back to Stuart. What about my car? Danny replies that I can come back down and get it later in the week.

"Okay. What the hell" This sounds like a great time and Mickey agrees.

We load up the limo: me, Mickey, Danny, Kimmy (who is Danny's manager from Vermont), Billy (one of Danny's bartenders), and Tony (the bouncer).

Two cars load up to follow us, and off we go. We take the back roads to get to the turnpike. In Boca we are about to go by a mall that has a TGI Fridays.

I look at Danny and say, "Let's stop for a round of shooters."

Danny agrees. So we pull in, and about twelve of us head into Fridays around 3:30 p.m. on a Wednesday afternoon. All of us are shitfaced, of course! We order a round and another after that.

Okay, back to the limo to continue our journey.

The two cars following us make the right decision to head back to Coral Springs, but on to the turnpike we go.

After about twenty-five miles we are in South Palm Beach. I turn to Danny and tell him there is a bar right off the turnpike exit called the Dark Horse Saloon, and I think we need another shooter. Off the turnpike we go. The limo pulls into the parking lot and we all spill out.

Going into the bar, everyone looks at us like that scene in the movie *Animal House* when they walk into the bar to see Otis Night!

I make a corporate decision and go to the bartender and tell him to give everyone a drink on us. After that, it's like we're regulars, with everyone hugging us and shaking hands like we grew up together.

Another couple of rounds of shooters and we are on our way back on the pike.

Right around the Jupiter exit, I tell Danny it would nice to stop at a restaurant in Jupiter on the waterfront so that I could get a scotch and watch the sun set, even though the sun sets on the other side of Florida.

Off the turnpike we go again, heading to Harpoon Louie's on the inlet in Jupiter. The limo pulls up in front of the restaurant, and we spill out again. The entrance to the restaurant has some nice plants and vegetation, so we admire the view and head in.

We barely make it through the front door. The manager and the hostess both immediately can see that we should not be served. They refuse to let us enter.

Well, Kimmy gets on her high horse and tells the two of them that we are all in the restaurant business, and that Danny owns three bars in Fort Lauderdale. He says we aren't driving, and we are ready to spend some money.

They still refuse to let us enter.

"Okay, screw you. We are outta here!"

On the way out, Tony takes a swing at one of the plants and knocks its head off!

As we try to get back into the limo, one of the cooks decides to come out and gets into Mickey's face. Billy and I can see that this confrontation is not going to go well. Billy picks up Mickey and carries him to the limo. We all get into the limo and head out of the parking lot and try to decide where the next drink will be. As we are crossing the draw bridge heading up US #1, I see not one, not two, not three, but four Jupiter cop cars heading south with sirens and lights blaring.

This can't be good!

Each of the four cars does quick U-turns and chase after us.

They pull us over just on the other side of the bridge. The limo driver puts down his window as one of the officers approaches. He talks to the driver for a minute, and then tells all of us to get out of the limo. One again, we all spill out, except for Billy. He remains in the limo, unnoticed by the officers. The next thing we know, we are lined up.

The manager and hostess from Harpoon Louie's are both in one of the cruisers.

One of the officers is putting his hand over our heads and the two girls from the restaurant attempt to identify us. It's starting to rain, so we are standing there in the rain while Billy sits in the limo making faces at us and drinking beer without any of the cops noticing. Finally, the car with the restaurant manager and hostess pulls away.

One of the officers takes one of us at a time into his car, to ask each one of us what happened at the restaurant. I am the last one.

When I get in to the car the police officer tells me not to give him any of the bullshit about being in the restaurant business and having a limo. He just wants to know what happened.

So I tell him, "Officer, I saw the whole thing. Tony took a swing at the plant and hit it, but if we had let the fight continue, I think the plant would have kicked the shit out of him".

The cop looks at me and says "Get the fuck out of my county, you and the rest of your crew and I don't ever want to see you again!"

Into to the limo we go ... and stop at the first bar we see.

It's The Plush Pony in Palm Beach County. Sorry officer. We walk into the bar. I know Pete, the bartender. He asks me if we were the ones in the limo on the side of the road he saw on his way in to work. I tell him it was us, so he buys us a round of shooters - just what everyone needed after our ordeal with the Jupiter cops.

A couple more with Pete and off we go to Harper's in Stuart. Last stop! We pull in, and Al, the owner, is there. He buys us a round. After a couple more, Danny and the crew decide to head back. I ask him if I can ride back with him so I can get my car. He won't let me! Off they go.

Now, I have to call my wife to come to get Mickey and me. Needless to say, she isn't very happy!

Two days later, my wife drives me 80 miles to Coral Springs to pick up my car. We get there and I don't have the keys. I left the keys home. So it's all the way back 80 miles to Stuart and 80 miles back to Coral Springs the next day to get the car!

Once again, my wife is not very happy.

I never found out how much Danny had to pay for the limo ride, but whatever it was, it was worth it ... if only for the laughs.

THE PURPLE PUB

The Purple Pub was in Williamstown Massachusetts, home of Williams College. I started going there when I owned PT's Pub in Bennington. The owner – Mary -- and I became good friends, and we would frequently bounce back and forth between our bars.

After I closed T.J. O'Carmody's, I moved to Myrtle Beach for a while. Mary came down for a visit with one of my former bartenders (who was, of course, from Hoosick Falls).

While they were visiting, I mentioned to Mary that I would like to move back to the Bennington area, and was looking into opening another bar. With that, Mary suggested that I come to work for her while I did my prospecting. I liked the idea and told her that I would be happy to do that and that I would guarantee I stayed with her for at least one year.

I wound up at her place, The Purple Pub, from which I have some good stories to share...

The Purple Pub was a very small bar with a small kitchen, but Mary did well for lunches and some late night munchies. The crowd was mostly locals during the day, but at night -- after 9 p.m. -- it was all Williams College students.

The place would fill up until last call at 1 a.m. As the only staff from 6 p.m. until closing time, I was a busy beaver – particularly from 10 p.m. to 1 a.m. Tuesday, Wednesday and Thursday nights.

On Fridays, I had a cook in the kitchen. On the other three nights, I was the bartender and cook too!

To get into Williams College, you can't be a dummy, but these kids needed to be educated about how to handle themselves at a bar ... especially, how to tip.

But I was just the one to train them.

On my first night, my first customer comes up to the bar and orders a $5 pitcher of Genesee, putting a fiver down on the bar.

Pouring the pitcher, and knowing that there isn't going to be a tip with the transaction, I put a little more head on the pitcher than I normally do, probably costing my first customer a couple of extra glasses of beer.

When he gets the pitcher, he immediately complains, telling me I don't know how to tend bar. I inform him that in fact I do know how to tend bar, and that I work for the house, and that the head is where the profit is for the owner.

He gives me a dirty look and walks away. I'm hoping he gets my message.

So about and half hour later, he is back at the bar, ordering another pitcher with a fiver, plus a dollar bill. And this time he is happier with the pour.

After doing the same thing with cocktails, it took me a couple of weeks to get those students trained. It even got it to the point where some would come up and ask for a drink and inform me that they were a little short, but that money was coming from Dad later in the week and they would take care of me then!

They usually did, because they knew if they didn't … they would be way back to the end of the line.

After a month there I also got them trained in the art of last call. Mary had a bell behind the bar that you were supposed to ring for last call.

I rang the bell for the first couple of weeks -- couldn't get their attention. They would always bug me for another round.

So one night I decided to get their attention, so as I was ringing the bell I was yelling "Last Fucking Call!"

I did this for about a week and got them trained, so now when I rang the bell, I didn't have to say a word, because they would all turn and look at me and yell "Last Fucking Call!"

Mary wasn't there when I was giving my lesson in last call etiquette, but she did show up on one Friday night late and I rang the bell. As I got my response from the students, I thought she was going to have a heart attack!

She told me I couldn't do that. I told her it was too late, I got 'em trained! It is amazing the bond I formed with the students, coming in to see me before their graduation and thanking me for the lessons I had taught them.

Obviously in a college bar, you have to be strict with the ID's. I had a couple of door-persons that worked with me, who were great. They knew the questions to ask that would throw the student off, like ...

1. Zodiac sign 2. Zip code 3. Height and weight.

Using a fake ID, these kids weren't paying attention to the little details and would always get caught!

One night around 6 p.m., I have four students come and order a pitcher, sitting at a table as far away from the bar they could get! Going to the table I didn't recognize any of them as regulars, so I asked for their ID's.

Three had ID's. One didn't.

They asked me if I could give them a few minutes, while they tried to find the fourth ID. Walking away, I watched them huddle up. I gave them a few minutes and went back to the table. It was a miracle! And they were able to produce another ID!

Checking the ID -- knowing it wasn't the student's -- I was going to give him a fair chance, so I asked him his date of birth. His response was, "Something, something, 1970!"

Shit! You gotta at least know the date! Obviously not a math major.

On your way boys!

A couple of Mary Stories:

I would start my shift on Fridays, at 6 p.m., so I would get there around 5:30 to help with the flip over.

Well Mary would put out Happy Hour food on Fridays around 3 p.m., so when I came in I would clean up the mess and throw out the leftover food: the cheese that was starting to curl, the crackers that were going soft, the vegetables that were rubber by now, and the dip that was getting warm.

Mary was never around when I did this, so I thought it was the right thing to do!

Well one day Mary is there, and she stops me from throwing everything out, and tells me to wrap everything and put it in the refrigerator.

OK, it's you bar!

I ask what she is going to do with it, and she says she will show me later.

Around midnight that night, Mary comes strolling in, one hour before last call. The placed is packed and I am running my ass off!

Well, she tells me to go to the fridge and get out the food I put away when I came in.

OK. I'm busy as hell, but it's your bar.

Well I put the food out on the bar and these college kids start woofing it down like there is no tomorrow.

I finally give last call and start my clean up. Mary is sitting at the bar having a cocktail while I am doing this. I turn to her and say, "Mary, I always thought that you were Irish, but I believe that you are Jewish. There is no way any Irish person would have put that food out for those kids to eat."

Mary turns to me, looks me in the eye, and says, "TJ, if I was Jewish, I would have charged them for the food!"

Touché

Another Friday night I come in and Mary is not around. I go to make my first drink and grab the bottle of vodka. Tipping the bottle up, I begin my pour. All of a sudden the vodka stops coming out!

I turn to Liz, the bartender and manager that I am relieving, and ask her what is going on? She tells me that Mary installed pourers on top of all the liquor bottles, to control the amount of the pour!

So for the rest of the night, I have to tip the bottle twice, to be able to give my regulars a decent drink. By the end of the night, my arm is tired! Mary comes strolling in around 12:30, just before last call, asking me to make her usual, which is vodka and club soda.

I grab the vodka bottle and go make her drink, pouring the shot. The pourer stops the liquid at the precise amount. Putting the bottle back, I finish making Mary her drink!

She looks at me and says, "Hey make me a real drink!"

Aha! My response was, "If it's good enough for the customers, it is good enough for you!"

The next day the pourers were gone!

Story #19

IS THAT BABSON?

T.J. O'Carmody's was a bar I had in Hoosick Falls, New York.

Yes, we're reaching back in time for another Hoosick Falls story:

Up the street from O'Carmody's was a little restaurant and bar called Babson's Café.

Jeff -- the owner -- was a good friend of mine and a very good customer at O'Carmody's.

Jeff closed his place around 2 a.m. on Saturday nights, which gave him plenty of time to come down and see me, because we didn't give last call 'till 4 a.m.

Well, Jeff comes in one Saturday night and I can see he already has a start on a good buzz. He sits down at the end of the bar and proceeds to having a few Grand Mariners.

The night is going pretty good, the band is great, and we're busy!

And at the bewitching hour I give last call, turn up the lights, and try to get everyone out of there without any stupid fights or altercations.

Things are moving along fine 'till I hear a thud.

I look across the room and see that Babson has fallen off his barstool, landing on the floor -- right in the pathway where everyone else is trying to use the restrooms before they head home.

In typical Hoosick Falls' fashion, no one pays any attention to the body on the floor. They just nonchalantly step over him like there's nothing unusual going on.

Body on the floor? No big deal.

But, as the respected proprietor, I can't just let a body lie there in the middle of the floor, so I grab the two door men and tell them to get Babson up. And, of course, they look at me – puzzled -- and ask where they are supposed to put the body.

So I look around the bar, trying to figure out where to put the Babson.

Then I see it!

Sitting there up against the wall in plain sight is a portable salad bar on wheels, which I had never used. It had a slab of plywood on top with a table cloth covering it. All I had ever used it for was a place for customers to set down their cocktails.

I say to the door men, "Just grab the salad bar and set Babson up on top of it and push it into a corner. We'll worry about him after we get everyone else out of here and get the place cleaned up."

I was figuring that he might sober up enough to wake up later, so that I could send him up the hill and home.

The other bartender, the waitresses, the doormen, and I clean up the place and then -- of course -- sit down to have a few cocktails.

After a few drinks, of course we completely forget about Babson, until we hear a big moan.

The good news was that he's still alive. The bad news is that we can't wake him up!

So in my infinite wisdom, I tell the two doormen that we have a handicap ramp ... the salad bar has wheels ... and that they are going to push Babson home.

They give me some objections, but I assure them that we will wait for them and have a few more cocktails when they get back.

I watch them.

Off they go wheeling Babson, while the rest of us have another round. They are pushing him up the street like he is on a stretcher.

Babson has a little beer belly on him, so he's bouncing around on that salad bar like a big bowl full of Jell-O!

Then, as they get about half way up the hill, one of Hoosick Falls Police cars approaches the bouncing body on the salad bar, in the middle of the road, at 5 a.m. in the morning.

The officer rolls down his window, looks at the two doormen and the bouncing body and asks, "Is that Babson?"

The doormen reply, "Yes, that is, in fact, Babson."

And with that, the officer rolls up his window and drives away.

(That kind of thing happens only in Hoosick Falls!)

Well, they get Babson up to his own establishment, where he has an apartment above his bar. They search his pockets, find his keys, open up the door, toss the body in, yell to his wife and then take off like bats coming out of hell.

When they get back, I ask if everything went alright. They both answered, "Yes, except for one problem."

I ask, "What the hell was that?"

Well, it turned out that the salad bar had those solid rubber wheels, and they had forgotten to unlock one of the wheels. Now the wheel was flat on one side.

I said, "Don't worry about that." (See, I was walking away from the lease in a couple of weeks and I could care less about the salad bar.)

And so for the next couple of weeks I put the salad bar in a corner and put a brick under the flat wheel, which kept it sturdy.

Then, just before the lease is up, Jeff Babson comes down to see me, because he has heard that I am leaving and he wants to purchase the salad bar.

He asks me, "How much?"

I reply, "$300."

He goes over to the salad bar and looks it up and down and notices the flat wheel.

"I'm not going to pay $300," he says. "I will give you $200. One of the wheels is flat!"

I look at him and say "You're going to give the full price after I explain to you how the wheel got flat."

And after I tell him the whole story, he can't get the $300 out fast enough.

Then a week later, Sue and I go to Babson's for dinner, and there is that salad bar in a corner, fully stocked ... with a brick under the tire.

This stuff only happens in Hoosick Falls.

Story #20

THE FUNERAL DIRECTOR

In my junior year in high school, my parents decided that I probably should go into the funeral business.

My sister, Marilyn, and brother in law, Alex, owned a funeral home in Bennington, Vermont. They knew I wasn't spending much time with my studies and was devoting most of my time playing sports, dating and partying. They decided I might need a career. I got an offer to work at the funeral home for the summer.

They would give me a car to go back and forth from Manchester to Bennington. I would do just about anything to get my own wheels, so the deal was made.

They started me off slowly that summer. I mowed the lawns and washed the cars and the hearse. Soon, I was driving for funerals, making removals, and doing the embalming. Everyone always asks me how I could do a job like that. I always explain that it was like being a doctor, except you don't have to worry about losing the patient.

I could never work in an emergency room. The people I worked on weren't screaming, and if they did, you got the hell out of the room.

After finishing high school, I took a year off from studies before I went to school to study Mortuary Science, just to make sure I was okay with being a funeral director. I survived the summer and headed off to Hudson Valley Community College for two years, after which I returned to Bennington, Vermont, to begin my career.

I lasted full-time for three years until I moved to Maryland with my wife. In those three years I came out with a few great stories. Here are a few:

THE BRIDE OF FRANKENSTEIN: It's a Halloween Party. My brother-in-law, Alex, is dressed as the Bride of Frankenstein and I am dressed as Groucho Marx.

After a few cocktails, everything is going great, until we get a phone call. Someone has died at the hospital. There isn't much refrigeration at the hospital, so they want the body removed immediately.

Alex, being the boss and dressed in a wedding gown, makes the corporate decision that I should go to the hospital with the hearse to make the removal. He will meet me at the funeral home to do the embalming.

So off I go as Groucho Marx to the funeral home to get the hearse and then to the hospital to get the body.

Well, you just can't back up to the morgue door and grab a body! You have to go to the nurses' station and sign the body out. You should see the look on the nurse's face when she looks up to see Groucho Marx ready to sign out the body.

After a couple of laughs, she hands me the paper work. I sign it and off I go to get my body.

I get the body on the stretcher and into the hearse. It's around 10:30 p.m. and its pitch black. I pull the hearse around to the back of the funeral home and stop at the ramp that leads into the morgue. I hop out of the hearse and start pulling the stretcher out. All of a sudden, the morgue door kicks open and standing there is the Bride of Frankenstein. If someone happened to be walking by I think they would have gotten the hell out of there. I can't stop laughing.

I would title the movie, "Groucho Marx Meets the Bride of Frankenstein."

WHERE ARE HIS COLORS? One of the last funerals I did before I moved to Maryland was for a young man who belonged to a motorcycle gang. We are busy at the funeral home and have three or four wakes going on at one time. We have calling hours one afternoon from 2 p.m. to 4 p.m. and then 7 p.m. to 9 p.m. for this young man.

The family brings in the clothes for him -- no suit, but instead jeans, a shirt, and a vest. I get him dressed and placed into the casket without the vest because it had skull bones and other designs that I didn't think were appropriate to display in the casket.

The family comes in around 1:30 p.m. to make sure everything is all right and to get settled before the calling hours start.

I'm standing in the hallway as they go up to check out the body, when the girlfriend comes running out, screaming at me, "Where are his colors?"

The only thing I'm thinking is that I didn't put enough make up on him. Not knowing what she means by colors!

She says, "The vest with his colors! Every biker has his vest with his colors!"

Thank God I didn't throw away the vest. I go back into the morgue and grab the vest. I explain to her we can't put the vest on right now, and that I will lay the vest over him, and then between calling hours, I will get the vest on him.

She settles down and agrees to that.

Everything goes by without a problem from 2 p.m. until 4 p.m. The family leaves, and I put the vest on our friend. The family returns at 6:45 p.m. for the evening calling hours and they get settled down.

Around 7:10 I hear it the familiar sound of a Harley chopper, and there isn't just one ... there are about twenty of them.

In come the bikers all dressed in their leathers and colors.

I can feel the friction between these people and the family, but everyone is being respectful until I notice two of the bikers at the open end of the casket, trying to get our friend to sit up, and a third one trying to put a beer in his hand. I run into the room and ask them to stop.

After the body has been embalmed, there is no way this fellow is going to sit up!

I get the bikers to back down. The family allows them to put a beer in the casket and everyone settles down. There are no more problems, except for the stream of bikers going in and out of the funeral home, having beers outside, and coming back in.

The next morning the funeral is at 11:00 a.m. Since we have multiple funerals going on, I will be the only funeral director working on this one.

The family is ready. The minister is ready.

But we have no girlfriend and no motorcycle gang. The family is frustrated and the minister is ready to walk out. All of sudden, though, I hear the familiar roar of twenty Harleys. In they come.

So I get everyone seated and get the minister, but I am still missing one of the gang, who is supposed to be a pallbearer! I ask where he is and am told he is out puking in the bushes probably because he had too much to drink the night before. I start the service without him.

In the middle of the service, the front door opens and he comes in. The guy in the casket looks better than he does. Somehow, we make it through the service and get the casket into the hearse.

Now for the fun part.

The burial is in Connecticut, about two and one-half hours away. The head of the gang comes up to me and says they are going to follow me in a procession all the way. Just what I want! Thinking fast on my feet, I tell him it is illegal to take a funeral procession across state lines, and I will meet him in Connecticut. He falls for it!

Off to Connecticut I go with all kinds of stories about what the motorcycle gang is going to do at the cemetery: (a) They will shoot a dog and throw it on the casket, or (b) they will stand around the casket and urinate on it.

And I'm going to be by myself. How am I going to prevent any of this from happening?

I pull into the cemetery and seek out the superintendent. No one else is here yet, so I want to get everything set. The casket is on the lowering device; the flowers are set; the chairs set up; and I'm ready for the family and the gang to show up. I ask the super for some help.

He replies, "I am a WWII vet and I don't do any lifting!"

Great! I drive the hearse over to the grave, find the vault guy, and give him a $20 to help me. We are getting everything done, and the super comes over and tells me that there were about thirty bikers here earlier and they said they would be back.

Great!

The family and the minister show up for the graveside service. No gang. We wait in the heat of the Indian summer with me in my black suit, sweating like a stuffed pig. The minister approaches me and informs me -- just as the minister at the funeral home -- that he has to be somewhere else pretty soon. To hell with the gang, I thought. Let's get started.

But then I hear the familiar roar of about thirty motorcycles. The minister waits until they arrive. I try to arrange everyone to one side of the casket so he can start.

The gang doesn't want to stand where I ask them to stand. Shit! It's going to start. I go over to the minister and tell him he can get started, and it might be in his best interest to be brief.

I think he says "Dominus Nabisco" and runs for his car.

I approach the family so they can leave. I will stay here to make sure the vault cover in put on and sealed. They inform me that they aren't leaving until the gang leaves. So I go over to the gang and tell them that I will take care of the rest of the arrangements.

"Hell no! We aren't leaving! We have to conduct our own service, and Joe's going to the store to pick up the beer!"

Okay, TJ, Now, what do you do?

I tell the head of the motorcycle gang that the vault cover has to be put on before they can conduct their service, and back I go to the super, asking him where the guys who are to fill in the grave? I'm informed that the two guys won't be there for another hour.

Shit! Back to the vault guy. I tell him that there's only him and me to lower the casket and put the cover on. I lower the casket and pull the straps out. He backs up his boom truck to the grave, with me directing him and the gang and family watching.

Normally, I would take off my jacket and do this job, but because the family is still there I have to follow our business motto, "Sincere and Dignified."

After we get the truck centered, the vault guy handles the hydraulics while I try to steer the vault cover to the cement vault, which has the casket in it. The cover probably weighs a couple hundred pounds. I am half way in the grave, steering the cover. Down it goes, slowly, one end on, and then the other to form a complete seal.

Thank God.

Crawling out of the grave, I go over to the family and tell them that the vault is sealed and there is no way the gang can do anything to the casket, so they can leave now.

"We aren't leaving till the gang leaves!"

Okay, but my Irish ass is out of here because there isn't anything more I can do. Off I go and run into some gang members coming back with the libations!

A couple of days later I run into one of the family members and I ask, "What happened?"

He tells me it wasn't too bad. The gang put things on top of the vault that meant something to them and the deceased, and a few of them did some eulogies. Then they filled in the grave without waiting for the super and his workers.

After that, the family and the gang exchanged hugs and handshakes and everyone went their way. That last my last funeral, until I ran my own.

AUNT LIL: When I first started working at the funeral home, Alex's parents, Ed and Olga Mahar, lived in an apartment above it.

Ed was getting along in years and was cared for by a nurse. One day, I get a message that we had a call. Someone had died and we had to make the removal. I go to the funeral home and start to put on my suit because you never drive the hearse or make a removal without having a suit on.

Alex comes in and tells me not to bother putting the suit on, and to go out to the garage to get the portable stretcher. I give him a funny look and ask what is going on.

He tells me that Ed has died, and Bill and I have to go upstairs to make the removal.

So Bill arrives and I tell him what is going on. Off we go, stretcher in hand, to make one of the shortest removals in history. We get Ed on the stretcher, go down the front stairs, turn right, go down the hall, and into the morgue. Bill and I do the embalming. The funeral is going to be in a couple of days.

The day of the calling hours comes, and Ed is laid out, the flowers are set, and Alex, my sister Marilyn, her kids and my whole family is there for a private visitation by family before the public is let in.

I am sent to a nursing home to pick up Aunt Lil.

Seems that Lil was related to Ed, but I am not sure how.

I arrive at the nursing home in the big Oldsmobile, probably one of the first cars in Bennington with air conditioning. I get the wheel chair out of the trunk and go to get Aunt Lil. I get her in the wheel chair, and, as she sits down, her dress goes above her knees.

Looking up at me, Lil says "The dress is too short."

I tell her it's okay, and I roll Lil out to the Olds and get her in the front seat. As she sits down, though, she says again, "The dress is too short."

"Lil, it's okay."

As I pull up in front of the funeral home, Marilyn comes out to help with Lil. As we get her out of the car, Lil looks up at Marilyn and tells her, "The dress is too short".

Marilyn tells Lil that it's fine. Marilyn and I get Lil into the funeral home and put her into a seat we have saved for her. As she sits down she again looks up at Marilyn and me and says, "The dress is too short."

Again, we both tell her that it is fine.

Lil sits there for a couple of minutes, and then asks if she can go to the casket to say a prayer. As Marilyn and I escort Lil to the casket, she lets out a scream, "Ed, take me with you!"

She proceeds to pass out, falling on the floor! This is in the early 70's, long before anyone knew about CPR. Lil is on the floor, and we are trying to make her as comfortable as we can. Someone calls the rescue squad, which is probably in its first year of existence.

Before that, they would call the funeral home.

The rescue squad shows up and hands me one of those bags to put over Aunt Lil's mouth to do CPR. While I am squeezing, they are bringing in the stretcher. Up goes Lil, and out we all go to the ambulance, while I'm squeezing the bag and Marilyn is following us.

We get Lil into the ambulance, and I am waiting for them to tell Marilyn and me that we can get out before they rush Lil to the hospital. But the door slams shut.

Shit!

We are off, flying down Main Street. We have to make a left at the main interaction called the Four Corners. Okay, left we go, but on two wheels! I'm sure we are going to flip over! But down the other wheels go, and we are speeding to the hospital. We make the rest of the way on all four wheels, and pull up to the hospital emergency entrance.

Out comes the emergency room crew. We get the stretcher out and off we go -- with me still squeezing the balloon -- into an emergency room. Finally, a nurse says she will take over, and I can get the hell out of there! Amen!

Marilyn and I pace around the waiting room until one of the nurses finally comes out and tells us that they did everything they could do for Aunt Lil, but unfortunately they weren't able to save her. We thank the nurse, call the funeral home with the bad news, and ask if someone can come to pick us up.

Marilyn and I are out in front of the hospital waiting for our ride when we are approached by a nurse who knew Marilyn. She tells us how sorry she is about Lil and that in the haste to try to save her they had to cut the pretty dress that Lil was wearing.

Marilyn and I turn to each other and we both say "That's okay. It was too short anyway!"

Story #21

<u>TO THE AIRPORT!</u>

When I had a bar in North Bennington, Vermont, I bought a used Limo and opened up Shamrock Limo for some extra income.

One year, on the Monday after the Super Bowl, I'm in the office doing paper work when I get a call about an airport run I am supposed to do for a couple, and I am late.

Shit! I go flying out the door to get the limo and head to the Albany, New York Airport, passing cars on corners, going as fast as I can.

All the while I'm trying to think about the excuses I am going to give the customers for being late.

I arrive at the airport in record time, park the limo right in front, and a police officer says, "You can't leave it there!"

I plead my case, telling him I am late, the customers are waiting, and I will be right out of here. This is before 9/11, so things are looser than they are today. He tells me to hurry up.

I run into the airport, looking all over the place for the couple.

I can't find them.

This is before cell phones, so I run to the pay phones to call the bar to see if the couple has found another way home. The bartender answers and I ask him if he has heard from the couple. He tells me he has, so I ask him what's going on, and he says, "You were supposed to take them to the airport you asshole, not pick them up!"

Shit!

I quickly arrange to get them to the airport by borrowing the car of a customer who is sitting at the bar, and have another customer drive them to the airport. I park the limo, head back into the terminal, and pray that the couple gets there in time for their flight.

I check on their flight. They are going to Philly. Okay, if they miss the flight, I will pay for any extra expenses, and obviously I am not going to charge them for the limo.

Now, it's just a waiting game. Please get here on time! Pacing, pacing. How much is this going to cost me? Please get here on time!

They finally arrive. I run to the car, carry their bags in, and apologize as many times as I can. I tell them they won't have to pay anything, and I will cover any extra costs. How bad can that be? They are only going to Philly. Up to the counter I go where they are checking in. The agent says they will make it to Philly and be on time to catch their next flight to Germany! Holy shit! If they miss that flight, it's going to cost me big bucks!

Thank God, they make it.

I was at the Albany Airport well ahead of their arrival time, when they returned from Germany, after telling myself, "To the airport, asshole."

Story #22

<u>A HUNTING WE WILL GO</u>

Back when I was in the fifth grade at St. Francis de Sales, November came rolling around, and with that comes deer season in Vermont.

Now, if you are a real Vermont red neck, deer season means more to you than Christmas. Well, all of my classmates are getting ready to go hunting with their fathers. I approach my father and ask him if he will take me deer hunting.

Let me explain first. My father was 40-years-old when they had me. There were four other kids before me. He lived for golf, so asking him to take me hunting was like asking him to go to the dentist.

After a quick "no" to the hunting idea -- and me in tears -- my mother steps in and says it might be a good idea to take me hunting one morning.

My father owned a used car lot at the time, and one of the vehicles was a 1948 Willie's Jeep. The Friday before opening day of deer season, my father had his mechanic go out to jump start the jeep and get it ready for the hunting trip on Saturday.

Saturday comes, and at the break of dawn, every one of my friends is in the woods with their dads.

Not me. We're still home!

At around 10 a.m. my father heads down to the car lot and picks up the jeep. He comes back to the house and loads my brother Mickey, my sister Patty, and me into the jeep. Mickey is riding shotgun, Patty and I are in the back. No seats, so we are sitting on the wheel wells. Every bump we hit, our heads are banging on the roof. Off we go, heading to Shaftsbury, Vermont, to get our deer.

We get to a dirt road in Shaftsbury and my father turns on to the road up the hill into the forest. As I said, Mickey is riding shotgun. In his hands is a pistol with no bullets, but he does have a pistol.

I'm in the back of the jeep with a rusty knife in my boot. My sister Patty has no weapon. She wouldn't at that time, because she's was girl.

As we head up the dirt road, my father beeps the horn, probably to scare the deer away. I figure there are three ways that we are going to get a deer:

1. A deer jumps out and my father hits it with the jeep! I don't think that's going to happen with the horn blowing!

2. Mickey jumps out of the jeep and hits a deer over the head with the empty pistol.

3. I jump out of the back of the jeep, run down a deer, and stab it!

We make it to the top of the hill. My father lets Mickey and me out of the jeep so we can take a leak. We get back into the jeep and head home.

So much for deer season!

Story #23

CLOSING CARMODY'S

When I knew I was closing TJ O'Carmody's in Hoosick Falls, I stopped serving food. I had to keep the bar open in the afternoon because off-track betting was on the other side of the building, and I would get customers in for a few beers while they were betting the races.

I needed a bartender who didn't need to make much money, because the horse players were pretty cheap! I had a guy in mind. His name was Point, and sometimes he worked as a bouncer for me on the weekends.

I hire Point, knowing that he never tended bar before, because the hardest drink he had to make was Bud in a bottle.

The bar is closing at the end of August, which is when the Saratoga Race Track is open, so OTB is the busiest it is all year. I know Point is a little bit of a horse player himself, but I don't mind him making his bets as long as he keeps an eye on the bar.

Well, one day I come in to take over the bar for the night shift.

When I get there, Point is pacing around like one of the horses at Saratoga!

I check around and make sure the ice is stocked, the juices are filled, and the usual stuff bartenders do when they are changing shifts. As soon as I tell Point that everything looks good, he bolts out the door!

He comes back about thirty seconds later and blurts out that he had a hot tip in the 8th race at Saratoga! I say great, how did it work out?

Point tells me the horse came in last, and by the way, there is only about $5.00 left in the cash register, because he needed some money to bet the race!

Then, out the door he boogies. I go over to the register, hit the open drawer button, and find about $5.00 in change. After the initial shock, I start laughing. You can't make this shit up.

I had back-up money in the safe, and Point came back in a couple of days to pay me back. Lesson learned.

Never let a horse player handle your cash register during Saratoga!

Irish Wakes

I did my own Irish wake at TJ O'Carmody's in Hoosick NY. I also did four other wakes for customers, two in Bennington at Carmody's, and one at Carmody's West and one in Carmody's in Florida.

The first one was for Pendy. He was a good customer, family friend and the local bookie.

The night of the wake we got Resuscitation Annie all dressed up to look like Pendy -- with the Irish hat he used to wear.

We set the casket at the end of the bar, with the kneeler, the candles, and the Mass card tray.

The party starts at 8 p.m. and the bar is packed with everyone showing their respects for Pendy.

I have this customer -- an attorney from NYC -- who does a great impersonation of Father Guido Sarducci, the priest on the early Saturday Night Live shows.

I get everyone's attention and the good padre starts the service.

Soon, there's not a dry eye in the bar, not because of their sorrow for Pendy, but because the Padre has everyone in stiches! He's awesome!

After the padre gets done, I have Pendy's pall-bearers come to carry the casket out of the bar. It's around 9 p.m., and there is still a full dining room.

At Carmody's we separated the dining room from the bar with a wall and French Doors up to the ceiling. You could see into the dining room from the bar and vice versa.

That night the bar was so packed that the people in the dining room couldn't see what was going on in the bar, because there were so many customers.

But I am sure they were able to see a casket going through the bar as the pallbearers hoisted the casket on their shoulders. The hearse is parked out front, and they are carrying the casket out the front to the hearse. When they get to the front door, the casket is too big to go through the door, so the pallbearers turn the casket sideways!

Across from Carmody's is another restaurant. They are having a busy night too. They have about six tables that sit in the front window and look right at Carmody's.

Imagine their surprise when they see a casket coming out my front door!

But, as the pallbearers turn the casket sideways, Pendy falls out onto the sidewalk! Laughing, the bearers grab Pendy, throw him back into the casket and put the casket into the hearse! Everyone comes back inside and the party goes on!

The second wake was for the principal of the local high school! We had a good time that night but, Pendy's was still the best.

The third Wake was at Carmody's in Florida. The lucky stiff was John Leonard, a local electrician and friend.

Not having the connections in Stuart that I had in Bennington with a funeral home, I had to improvise.

For the casket I found a store in Delray that sold caskets, retail! Well I borrow a van and make the hour trip to Delray.

Lucky me I was able to purchase a lovely Kelly-green casket for around $350!

For the body in the casket we were able to get a store mannequin and did a pretty good job of getting the mannequin to look like John. I brought the prayer cards and guest book down with me from Vermont.

The night of the wake, John and his wife got into it. She is the merry widow and he is the deceased attorney. The party is going great, and it's time for the eulogy. John gave his own, as the attorney. He did a great job cracking everyone up.

It was time for the bearers, and as usual they wanted to carry the casket out on their shoulders. Not having the connections, I didn't have a hearse out front, but had a van ready for the casket to be put in. Well, as the bearers carry the casket out the front door, again it is not wide enough and as they jockey the casket around, they scratch the shit out of the top of my brand new casket!

Oh what the hell! We all head back in to party!

The fourth and final wake was at Carmody's West in Hoosick NY.

This was the scene: We're burying my former partner and good friend Kevin!

We get Annie back and get her dressed up as Kevin, with his Green Bay Packers hat on. He looks great. Back where I had connections at the funeral home we are able to get the casket and everything we needed to go with it with cards and guest book included.

As usual, the bar is packed and everyone is having a great time! A couple of Kevin's friends deliver eulogies and I give one too, but the eulogy that brought the house was done by Kevin's step-daughter.

She really roasted him! This time the casket went out the front door fine!

Then back into the bar to finish the night.

These crazy promotions are probably what I miss about not running my own bar, but I still do have the memories!

Story #24

CRAZY BAR PROMOTIONS

When I started at Harpers in 1981, Monday Night Football was in full swing.

Howard Cosell was one of the announcers for the telecast. You either loved

Howard or you hated him! Most people hated him!

I came up with a great idea:

Why not have a Hate Howard Night at the bar. Special drink prices, free food at half-time

Plus, everybody would get a ticket on a chance to throw a brick at Howard Cosell.

One of my good customers owned a TV store, so I was able to get a used TV from him for nothing! So on that Monday night, we set up the TV in a corner of the bar.

Everyone who comes in for the game gets a ticket for a drawing to throw the brick at the TV and take out Howard! The night is going great, and we are busy.

As halftime approaches, we do the drawing.

This cute, petite young lady was the winner. Howard always came on half time to give his rundown of the games that were played on Sunday. I give the young lady the brick and position her a couple feet in front of the TV.

Everyone is waiting for the commercials to end and for Howard's face to appear on the TV. All of a sudden there he is and the young lady lets the brick fly. She takes off the left side of Howard's face and the TV implodes!

The owner, worrying about a fire from the implosion uses the fire extinguisher on the TV!

Not very smart.

The fumes drove everybody out of the bar! End of Promotion!

Buses to Saratoga

The first time I took a bus to the Saratoga racetrack was when I owned P.T.'s Pub in Bennington, Vermont. I had been involved in some bus trips when I worked at Danny's, but I never set up my own.

I rented a Vermont Transit Bus (not being smart enough to know if I rented school buses, it would have been much cheaper), and I filled the bus with willing participants.

My big mistake, after not living up North for a while and forgetting Saratoga's schedule, was that I booked the trip on Travers Day, the busiest day of the year at Saratoga.

We arrived in time but the place was crazy. I had plenty of beer and food on the bus, which was a good move because it took us two hours to get out of the parking lot!

The next time I ran trips to Saratoga was out of Hoosick Falls.

I would only rent a 15 passenger bus and hire a driver, so it was easy to control.

One night, however, we come back from the races get to the parking lot, start to unload the van, and we hear some moaning!

We look around and find a body lying on one of my volleyball courts.

Luckily, I had Sue with me, who was an ER nurse at the time. One of the other women was also a nurse, so both of them jump in to help this guy, while I call 911.

The Rescue Squad comes right away and they rush the guy to the hospital. We find out later that the guy had been drinking at a bar up the street and became friendly with a female customer. She asked him to leave with her and when they got out side, she and her boyfriend jumped the guy, stole his money, beat the shit out of him, and left him to die.

If we don't show up? He dies!

The next time I do the buses is at T.J. and Mike's in North Bennington. This time I rent school buses.

That day would start for me at 5 a.m. I go down to the bar and meet a couple of guys who are going on the trip. I have a truck and we load it up with beer -- at least half a case for everyone on the bus, and then we load the food.

The three of us then head to Saratoga, an hour away. We pull up to the track and I explain to the security guards that I am bringing over a group on a bus later and I am there to drop off the beer and food. They give us fifteen minutes to go in and unload everything.

After unloading, I leave the two guys there to watch over the beer and food until I return with the bus full of customers.

We park the bus, and everyone follows me to the location where I had left the two guys to guard the food and beer. It was usually a good time with plenty of food and beer. I always prided myself on never running out of beer when I did a promotion.

These trips always had their glitches, but there are a few that stick out:

When I bought the Shriners bus, I would use it for the trip to Saratoga along with a rented school bus. When the races got done, I would load up the school bus with the older customers and those who had had enough, and send that bus back to Bennington.

I would then load up my bus and go to downtown Saratoga as if everyone hadn't had enough to drink. Let's go to more bars for three more hours! The last call to get back on the bus to Bennington was 9 p.m. at the Parting Glass Pub, an Irish bar in Saratoga.

On one trip I had Joe attached to my hip for the whole day. Joe knew I always bought drinks for everyone and he wasn't going to get very far from me because he didn't want to miss out on the free drinks.

Joe's daughter worked for me, doing the books. So on this trip it's now 9 p.m., and for some strange reason Joe is not on my hip.

I start loading the bus and it's now 9:20 and no Joe!

Everyone on the bus is getting antsy. It's 9:35 and no Joe. Everyone wants to leave. Finally, at 9:45, after being told by the cops to move the bus, and going around the block four times, I pull the plug.

Shit! How am I going to explain to Joe's daughter that I left her father in Saratoga, with more than his share of cocktails in him?

As I am worrying about this, fifteen minutes into the bus ride, a domestic fight breaks out on the bus. I jump in and break it up, move the wife to the front of the bus and leave the husband in the back, and I stand in the middle of the bus until we get back to Bennington, to prevent further violence.

We get to the four corners in Bennington, and I tell everyone on the bus that they are not allowed in the bar. They have had enough to drink and it's time to go home.

I unload the bus in the front of the bar and pull the bus out back to unload what is left of the beer and food. I assume everyone has gone home. I head into the bar and to my surprise, everyone I told to go home, including the fighting couple, is in the bar.

I look at everyone and scream, "I thought I told you all to go home."

They look back at me and say, "We didn't think you were talking about us!"

Now I am pissed and give last call.

The drunks who have been with since 10 a.m. this morning can't understand why I am pissed! It's 11 p.m. and time to go home? I get everyone out and head home, worrying about Joe and wondering how I am going to explain to his daughter that I left him in Saratoga.

I get up the next day and head into the bar around 7 a.m. I want to have the paper work done, before I explain to Joe's daughter about her father.

As I arrive at the back door of the bar -- with the police station is right behind it -- I hear someone yell good morning to me. I turn to see who it is. It's Mr. Domestic being escorted in handcuffs to the police station.

He yells at me, "Hey TJ! Had a great time yesterday."

You gotta be kiddin' me!

The final drink Mr. and Mrs. Domestic had at the bar before I threw them out last night apparently didn't work out well.

I go inside, do the paper work and wait for Joe's daughter to show up for work. When she gets there I ask her if she has talked to her dad. Her response is "No, why?"

"Well," I told her. "I left him in Saratoga last night."

"What?"

She calls her mother. The good news is that Joe is home. He must have gone outside to get some fresh air last night and got lost. By the time he got back to the Parting Glass, the bus was gone. Joe got a taxi to take him back to Bennington, with no money. Joe had to hit the ATM to pay for the taxi, $100.

I gave Joe's daughter the rest of the day off and vowed to myself that I would never do a late bus from Saratoga again.

But I did it again the next year!

<u>HOLE IN ONE</u>

I've played golf most of my life and I've made two holes in one. Well, really, only one and one half!

In the late seventies I'm playing a practice round for the spring tournament at Mount Anthony Country Club in Bennington, Vermont. We get to the fourth hole. It's a short par 3, about 114 yards, so it's a wedge or sand wedge for most players.

My partner for the tournament goes first and knocks it up close to the green. I am next and take my usual dippy swing and hit the shot fat! It goes around twenty feet, so my partner tells me to hit another one -- a Mulligan.

We're only playing a practice round, so I drop another ball and make a much better swing and watch the ball sail towards the green. I think it's going to be close! The ball bounces, then rolls up to the hole, and it goes in!

Awesome! A hole in one!

But, no, not officially. It's really a par and it's not even that, because I didn't declare the ball to be a provisional!

Shit!

I don't care. It's a hole in one to me, and I'm buying drinks! We celebrate anyway, but I never did get credit for the hole in one.

The other hole in one happened in Florida in the mid-eighties.

I'm playing with my brother, Mickey, and a visiting pro from Ireland. We are playing the Gold course at Mariner Sands in Stuart, Florida. I am not having a good day, but any day on the golf course is a good day!

We reach the par 3 15th hole. The wind is in our face and the shot is around a 160 yards. With the breeze blowing in, I take a four iron and let it fly. It's looking good and I think it might be close.

It rolls in!

Mickey, the Irish pro, and I give high fives. A real hole in one! Well, we finish the round, with me going *bogey ... actually double bogey, bogey, double bogey*. Who cares? I had a hole in one. You know the rules! When you get a hole in one, you are supposed to buy a round for everyone.

When we finish, the Irish pro says he has to leave. I turn to Mick and say, "If he's not going in, neither are we. Those guys in there can buy and sell me.

"You and I are going to celebrate, but we are going to do it where I can afford to do it!"

So Mickey and I go to the nearest bar and celebrate my hole in one.

I never got that one fully recognized either, but I don't care. The Irish Pro, Mickey and me -- we know I got one!

<u>ONE TRIP TO Ireland</u>

I have been lucky enough to go Ireland twice, once when I owned P.T.'s Pub and again when we opened up Carmody's Downtown.

These are stories from those two trips:

The first time I go over with five other people.

All of us are in the bar business. We have drinks at P.T.'s Pub around noon before we head to the airport. We get to New York around 4 p.m., and head to a bar owned by a friend of my buddy Danny from Fort Lauderdale, Florida.

We start drinking there while watching football games. After three hours of good drinking we head to the airport. The flight is around 11 p.m. We spend a little while at the bar in the terminal.

We've been drinking all day, so why stop now?

No one is paying attention to the time and all of a sudden you hear a bell ring and the bartender tells us that if we don't get our asses going we're going to miss the flight. The bartender tells me that they always ring the bell for the plane to Ireland because everyone is drinking before the flight, and nobody would make the flight if they didn't kick people out.

We board the plane and get settled. As soon as we level off and the seatbelt sign is off, it's time to order more drinks. Aer Lingus wants to get you drunk quick, hoping you will sleep most of the way.

But none of us are going to sleep! Let's play liar's poker! We play until we know the numbers on all the bills by heart. The flight attendants urge us to be quiet and get some rest. No way. We are too pumped up. So we start telling jokes for a while, and the flight attendants still aren't happy with us. We do finally dose off but not for long.

We have arrived.

We make it through customs, and then head off to get our three rental cars that came in a package deal. None of us are within the limit to drive, but they give us the cars anyway. Two of the cars go to Jury's Hotel in Dublin. I am off to play golf at Portmarnock Golf Club, and drive the car on the wrong side.

With a few mental adjustments, I get the car under control.

After playing 18 holes and walking with a caddie, I have sobered up, thank God.

When we finish I ask the caddy to take us to his favorite watering hole. I really want to see a real Irish pub. He takes us for a beer to an old garage with the oil pit still in place.

So much for a real Irish pub!

We head to Jury's to check in and catch up to the others. At the hotel, I just want to go to the room and catch up on some sleep. The crew isn't going to let me get away with that, though, so after a quick shower we are off to drink our way through Dublin.

We hit some pubs and find some time to have a meal, and end up back at Jury's main bar around 10 p.m. The bar only stays open until 11 p.m., but they do have a smaller bar that stays open until 1 a.m.

You need to show your key to get in. Around 10:45 we gather many of the drunks that we have been talking with and head to the smaller pub.

The party rolls on!

The bartenders at the small bar are getting to like us. All of us are in the business, so we are tipping with every round, which they don't do in Ireland. Now, they are loving us! At last call I ask the bartenders if they will go out after work for a drink. They tell there are wine bars that stay open and they will meet us at one for a drink.

The six of us get directions and head out to get a cab to take us to the wine bar. Problem! The party has grown by one. A couple joined us somewhere along our journey that night. They were on their honeymoon. At last call, the husband had sent his wife to their hotel room and he's coming with us.

Outside the hotel we try to get a cab, but they won't take seven passengers. Instead of splitting up and taking two cabs, I come up with the great idea. I will drive the seven of us in my small rental car with the steering wheel on the wrong side.

I only have been drinking for about 36 hours straight.

All seven of us pile into the car, pull out of Jury's, and head to the wine bar. I make the first left hand turn and head right into traffic.

Holy Shit!

Somehow we make it to the wine bar, but I have to parallel park the car. I bump the car behind me, and when I look out the window there is a police officer standing there.

He request that I roll down my window. In my haste to do that, and being on the wrong side of the car, I turn on the windshield wipers and spray the officer.

Now, he asks me to get out of the vehicle.

Out I go and then he asks me "You had a bit of a bang with the car behind you?"

I tell him I think I had a bit of bang with the car in front of me too. He looks at all three vehicles and sees there is no damage. He comes back to me and asks if I am a Yank. I reply that I am, and he tells me to leave the car there for the night and to not drive again.

I thank him and tell him I will not drive again. Off we go into the wine bar to meet up with the bartenders from

Jury's. After an hour or so, I have enough, so I try to round up the troops. No one wants to leave. Screw them!

Out I go to my little car, and down the road I go with a couple of my crew chasing me with my arm out the window and my finger in the air!

I don't know how I found my way back to the hotel, but the next morning we go out to the rental and the passenger-side door is caved in.

We drive the car like that for the next couple of days. When we return it to the airport, park it with the damaged door along a fence, and hope no one will notice it.

Just about then, along comes one of the attendants, who looks at the door.

He says, "You had a bit of a bang with the car. You need to go inside and fill out a report."

We tell him we will, and head straight to the terminal. Three months later I get a bill for over $400 for door repair. What the hell. It was worth it for the story.

Three months later, I get a phone call from the bartender at Jurys. He says that they want to know when we are coming back. They miss us!

Another story from Ireland:

The second time over there I went with my two brothers, two nephews and some good friends.

Just the 12 of us went over to Ireland to play golf, see the sights, and maybe, have a few pints.

We arrive in Dublin and head down to Killarney, where we will be staying for a couple of days. After taking a nap, we all head out for our first round of golf. After the round and a few pints we head to Killarney to hit the pubs.

We are traveling in a van, so we have the driver drop us off in the center of town. Having a great time, we are in a pub when they give last call around 11 p.m.

They throw us out into the streets with a crowd of Irishmen milling around. No one wants to go back to the bed and breakfast. Having been in Ireland before, I know that there has to be a place where we can keep the party going. I turn to one of the drunken Irishmen standing next to me. I ask him if there is an after-hours bar.

He tells me to go down this alley. Knock on a door there. Inside is a bar, but there's a cover charge of $10 a head. Hell, we don't care. We're in Ireland. Keep the party going!

We head down the alley, knock on the door, give the guy eighty bucks and head in. Damn! It's the same bar they just threw us out of. As a matter of fact, my Johnny Walker Black is still sitting on the bar! What the hell! I go over, grab my drink, and we party until they throw us out again.

Outside the bar, we flag down a cab -- a van -- to get all eight of us home.

I'm a little claustrophobic, so I sit in the front seat. I get stuck with the cab fare -- the cabbie charges me $20, so I give him $25.

The next day we go through the same routine of golf and the pubs until last call. We take the same cab. Same fare!

On our last day in Killarney we play golf. We're a little tired, so we decide to have a quiet dinner and then get a good night's sleep. After dinner we hit one pub and we just can't rally. So off we go to the bed and breakfast. The same driver picks us up again (probably the only van in Killarney). I am in the front seat again.

When we get there I reach for the usual $25. The driver says the fare is $10! I ask him why, since the last two nights the fare was $20?

His reply, "I charge you more when you are drunk!"

I say, "Thanks for being so honest. Here's $25!"

POP-A-SHOT

I brought the first Pop-a-Shot basketball game to Vermont.

A vending company provided a juke box, pool table, and video games. The split was 50/50. That was okay because when there was a problem, they fixed it, and if a game wasn't doing well they exchanged it for another.

When I told this vendor I was buying my own game, he tried to talk me out of it, saying it would break down and I wouldn't be able to fix it; I wouldn't be able to get parts.

Screw him.

I know the money this game can make. The game arrives and we get it set up, but before I can use it, it has to be inspected by the liquor authority.

The liquor authority? What do they have to do with a Pop a Shot game?

Anyway, two officers show up and check out the game. We have the machine placed so the player would have his back to the bar. These two officers told me that they want me to rearrange the machine because they are worried about balls bouncing out of the game and down the bar, knocking over drinks. That would lead to fights!

Are you kidding me!

We rearrange the machine. The officers are happy and leave. Well, I am telling you, this game made a ton of money! I had Pop a Shot nights, with teams playing for prizes. Kids who were in for something to eat with their parents would play. It was crazy.

The only maintenance I have to do on the game is one relay switch on the hoop to count the balls that went through. I find a supplier for that part and change it myself.

One of my stories about the machine is about one of the town drunks. One afternoon I am tending bar and he comes walking in. I won't serve this guy. I think he went to the ER room once and registered a blood alcohol level so high he should have been dead.

He walks up to the bar and asks for a beer. I tell him I won't serve him. He makes a face and looks like he is going to start to argue with me, but then he notices the Pop a Shot game, and starts to tell what a great basketball player he was for the Bennington Catholic School.

Growing up, I knew all the players on those teams and I guarantee he wasn't one of them.

So I tell him if he can beat the top score on the game I will buy him a beer. I even give him the fifty cents to play the game.

He accepts the challenge.

The customers and I crowd around the machine, and the drunk gets ready. In go the two quarters and the timer starts. He starts throwing up balls, and he did not make one basket.

I have seen little kids play the game and at least get a couple of shots through the hoop, but I had never seen anyone not make at least one shot.

The look on his face is great. He can't believe it! I asked him what the hell happened.

He replies "They played a box and one on me, and I couldn't adjust to the defense!"

We all started to laugh. I brought him over to the bar and bought him a beer. He really needed it!

I Have Been Smacked

During all of the years I have been in the bar business, I have been hit only twice. I jumped the bar a bunch of times and would get in the middle of the scrum and break up the fight. Most of the time the participants would recognize me and the fight would break up. I would then decide if I would throw anyone out.

One night I could see two guys were going to get into it and I didn't have time to jump the bar. I was making a drink at the time.

Thinking fast, I take the soda gun and squirt both of them with water. They both look at me and ask what the hell I'm doing?

I tell them that I am putting out a fire and, if they don't go separate ways, I will have both of them thrown out, and banned for life!

With that, they settle down.

Another time I'm at P.T.'s Pub. It's a Saturday night in early spring. It's warm and everyone is out. After a long winter they can't wait to get outside.

The bar is packed and I make the mistake of having only one bouncer on, because I can feel the friction around 11 p.m.

I know something is going to happen.

After being in the business for so long, you get that sixth sense, and you know when something is going to happen. Well it does, and it is a big one. They are fighting everywhere. I can't jump the bar because my bouncer has been knocked down in the corner where I was working, and if I jump the bar I will land on him.

I look over and notice a black guy kicking my downed bouncer. I run around the bar as fast as I can, and with help we get the fight outside. The cops show up and help break everything up.

One of the pain-in-the-ass cops tells me I have to close down.

I turn to his supervisor, knowing that he is not right, and ask him if I have to close down. He tells me I do not have to close for the night. I turn to the pain in the ass and give him a smile.

[141]

But I do go back in the bar, take the microphone from the DJ and announce that we are closed. I want everyone to know that we will not stand for this type behavior. Everyone grumbles, but they leave, knowing that I will not allow what happened tonight happen again.

As for the bouncer, the cops take him to the ER, take pictures of his bruises, and I give them the name of the black guy who was kicking him.

Two months later they put the black guy on trial and find him innocent!

Back to the two times I got smacked. Each time it was by a woman and both times it was at P.T.'s Pub.

The First Time: There was another town drunk, who supposedly had tried to commit suicide. Obviously it wasn't successful.

The bullet was still in her head, and made her a little unstable. I am tending bar one afternoon and she comes walking in. She asks me for a drink and I tell her I am not going to serve her and that she has to leave.

She tells me that she is not going to leave, so around the bar I go.

Getting in her face, I start walking her to the front door. I get her to the door, open it up, and ask her to leave. She tells me she won't go through the door because -- she says -- as soon as she is in the door, I will push her down the stairs.

After a couple of minutes of arguing and telling her I am not going to push her, I tell her I will go out first, and then she can follow me. She agrees to this proposition. So out I go, making the step down to the street, and the next thing I know she has jumped on my back and she's slapping me on the head!

What a dummy I am! I finally get her off me, and with a smile on her face she walks away.

The Second Time: It's just before Christmas and the funeral home crew is going to come in for a few cocktails before they go out for their Christmas dinner.

This will be the first time my sister Marilyn will be in P.T.'s Pub, so I want to make it a good experience. I have cheese and crackers ready for them. The place is decorated for the holidays and looks great.

They arrive and are sitting at the bar and having a good time. I have only one problem. I have this drunk female sitting in a booth, saying, "f---in" this and "f--in" that.

I go over to the table and realize she is from one of the toughest families in Bennington. They are well known for their escapades. This isn't going to be easy, but I tell her and her friends that they have to leave, and she refuses!

I am able to convince a couple of guys it would be better if they got her out of there instead of me calling the police. They convince her to go, but not without her making a scene.

Everyone is watching as the guys start taking her to the front door. I open the door so they can get her out. Just as she is almost out the door she turns back and kicks me square in the balls!

As she is laughing, the guys pull her out, and as I am closing the door and saying in my highest voice ever, "And you have a good night!"

Everyone has a good laugh, and back to their cocktails and their conversations.

Me? I go into the office and rub my balls for about half an hour!

Story #28

ROAD TRIP IN A HEARSE

After I graduated from high school, I worked full time for a year at a funeral home in Bennington, Vermont. That was before going to Hudson Valley Community College in Troy, New York, to get my degree in mortuary science.

In Vermont at the time, if anyone died of suspicious reasons, the body had to go to Burlington for an autopsy, done by the State Medical Examiner.

One day, I got to make the three hour 120-mile trip to Burlington from Bennington on US Route 7, a two lane highway.

I head out early one morning with a body, and arrive at the morgue in Burlington around 11a.m. The morgue attendant tells me they won't have the autopsy done until around 4 p.m., so I have 5 hours to kill in Burlington.

There are maybe five colleges in the Burlington area: UVM, Champlain, St. Michael's, and a couple of others. I have friends who attend some of them, so off I go to see if I can find any of them.

Well, a couple of my friends rent a house together in downtown Burlington. I have an idea where the house is, so I head down there with the hearse, wearing my black suit. I find one of them at the house and we decide to go to lunch, or should I say, go have a liquid lunch. Let the party begin!

After a few beers, we head back to the house and stop on the way to pick up a supply of beer for a house party.

Around 3 p.m. classes end and friends show up at the house. The party is getting bigger. Now, I have to make a decision. I've had a few drinks. Do I drive the hearse back to Bennington with a body in the back?

It is January, and it looks like a few inches of snow will fall soon. I make a corporate decision and call the funeral home to tell them I'm nervous about driving the hearse in the snow storm. I don't want to slide off the road with a body in the back. It wouldn't look good for the business.

Bill, who took the call, knows I'm full of shit and just want to stay in Burlington to party. But he makes arrangements for me to leave the body over night at a funeral home in Burlington.

At 4 p.m. I go to the morgue, pick up the body, and bring it to the Burlington funeral home for the night.

Then back to the party!

When I arrive, I park the hearse in front of the house. Inside the party house, we notice an old lady who lives across the street. She keeps peeking out her window to stare at the hearse.

We decide to give her a show.

We carry one of my buddies out of the house like he is dead and throw him in the back of the hearse. Three of us hop in the front seat of the hearse for a ride around

Burlington. At traffic lights, one of my buddies rolls down the window and yells at pedestrians, "You know we're going to get you."

The guy in back pops up and waves to them. We get a lot of funny looks.

We return to the party house to party into the wee hours. I wake up early, put on the black suit, and go to get the body to drive to Bennington. When I arrive at the Burlington funeral home, I don't look too well and I smell like a brewery. No one says anything, and off I go with the corpse.

Less than an inch of snow fell the night before and the roads are clear. When I get back to Bennington, Bill gives me a little shit about the stunt I pulled.

It was worth it.

SHAMROCK LIMO

When I owned T.J. & Mikes Place in North Bennington, I had an itch to own a limo.

So one day I took off on a road trip to Massachusetts and came back with a white, six-passenger Lincoln limousine. It was a great car and it got plenty of use for weddings, proms, airport runs, and of course personal use.

One day, I am at a bar having a few cocktails, when I start talking with a couple of regulars. These guys are involved with the Shriners, and always participate in my St. Pat's parades.

They ask me if I would like to buy a bus. A bus? What the hell am I going to do with a bus?

They reply that I have a limo, so why not a bus? After another drink, I ask them if it's the bus they put in the parade, and how much do they want for it?

They tell me it's the same bus, and it has 22 seats, a bar and a restroom.

Twenty two seats, a bar and a restroom? This sounds like fun. Okay, how much? They reply, "$1,500."

I tell them my father was a used car salesman, and if they want $1,500, he would tell me to offer them $1,000 and then we would meet in the middle at $1250! They look at me and reply that they will take the $1,250.

Holy Shit! Now, I own a bus?

I pick up this bus the next week. I'm driving it, even though I don't have a bus driver's license. The first place I take my bus is to a friend of mine who paints cars.

After some negotiations and some trade outs for bar privileges, we are going to get the sucker painted a nice Kelly green with the Carmody's logo on both sides.

We had a great time in that bus. I used it for golf outings, outings to races at Saratoga, weddings and parades.

Bus Story:

A couple of ladies from New Jersey show up at Carmody's and inquire about the limo for a wedding. They need a stretch that handles fourteen passengers.

I tell them that I only have a six passenger limo, but I have a bus that has 22 seats a bar and a restroom. They say they will take it.

I tell them I think it's best that they take a look at it first. It's not a rock star bus. I give them the directions to find the bus and look it over.

To my surprise, they call and tell me that they want to use it. They give me a date and I give them a price. Everything is all set.

Wedding day arrives. The bridal party needs to be picked up at a bed and breakfast in Dorset, Vermont, then brought up to Stratton Mountain to the Chapel of the Snow, and then back to Dorset after the wedding ceremony.

No problem!

I decide I will do the run, even though I still don't have a license to drive the bus. I put on my tux and head up to Dorset.

Dorset is a little town with money problem. They have too much of it. They think they are better than most, so pulling up in this big, green, 1973 school bus should turn some heads!

It's a beautiful day, and I arrive at the bed and breakfast right on time. As usual for a wedding, they are running late. We finally get everyone loaded in the bus. They bring champagne and food for the ride after the wedding.

The bride is riding to the wedding in a van with her maid of honor and will meet us at the Chapel of the Snow. Before we take off, the bride comes up to me and asks if I will take the back roads up the mountain to avoid the traffic in Manchester. She wants everyone waiting at the chapel for her to arrive.

I tell her that's no problem. I know every back road in Manchester, because I used to go parking on them when I was in high school!

You aren't going to go very fast when you take a 1973 bus full of passengers up a mountain. I make it to the narrow two lane axis road to Stratton. I go up the road as fast as I can, which isn't very fast. I look in the rear view mirror and see the van with the bride. There is nowhere for them to pass, so they hang on my bumper.

I reach the driveway to the chapel and pull in.

I am getting everyone off the bus when the bride comes running over, yelling "I told you to take the back roads! I wanted everyone waiting for me!"

I tell her I did take the back roads and that the bus doesn't go up mountains very fast, but to relax. After the service we will go down the mountain very fast, because it doesn't have any brakes! She looks at me, and then breaks in to a laugh.

I tell her to go get married and we will have a good time after! They had a great time coming down the mountain, and the wedding was a success!

DUMB CUSTOMERS

Being in the bar business for over 35 years, you get to see some really dumb people. Any time you throw in some booze and possible some other substances they become even more dumber. Here's an example:

One winter night at P.T.'s Pub I am running a Pop a Shot Tournament. It's a slow Wednesday and I have about ten of us playing the game and having a few beers.

The front door opens up and I look over to see a couple of Vermont woodchucks coming in. Right away I notice that they probably already have had enough to drink.

Making eye contact with the bartender, I let him know that we aren't going to serve the new arrivals.

I watch as the bartender explains to them that he thinks that they have had enough to drink and that he can't serve them tonight.

They start making a little ruckus, so I go over and introduce myself, and tell them that I am the owner. I appreciate their business; but that the law says I can't over serve customers and it looks like that they have a few before they got there. They aren't too happy with me, but I am able to escort them out the front door.

Back to the Pop a Shot game. I look outside and see the two dummies milling around their beat up pickup truck. One of them pulls out a chain saw!

Holy Shit! They are going to try to chainsaw the front door! I yell over to the bartender to call 911, to let the police know that we have two bozo's getting ready to chainsaw the front door.

I watch the two donkey's for a couple of minutes. They can't get the saw going. They jump in the truck and pull away. A couple of minutes later the cops show up and I give them a description of the truck. The police have a general idea who these two idiots are.

As the cops pull away to look for these guys, the two idiots pull in front of the bar again!

They jump out and try to start the saw again. The cops, having done a U-turn, pull up right behind the truck. While the idiots are still trying to start the saw, they don't notice the cops standing there! The cops just wait until they get the saw started, then walk over and arrest them!

You would think after you didn't get the saw started the first time, it's time to go home. But no, these idiots decide to go down the block, prime the saw, get it going, and come back. If they only go home they won't have to spend quality time with the police.

Well, how much wood can a Vermont woodchuck, chuck?

LONGEST PUTT EVER!

Since the early '90's I have been putting with a long putter. After trying to go side saddle, closing my eyes, holding the shaft against my left arm and whatever other stupid way I could think of to putt, I grabbed a long putter one day at a golf store and have been putting with it since.

Even though the USGA and the Royal and Ancient have put a ban on my long putter, I am still using it. Ok, Ok, I am not anchoring the putter, but after over 20 years of using the long one, I can't go back to the short one.

I would use that putter from everywhere! On the green, off the green, in the sand traps anywhere I had to chip, 'cause my chipping was deadly (by that I mean, if you stood on the green while I was chipping, I would probably zing one at you and cause you bodily harm!).

My brother Jack gave a name to the shot I would do off the green. He called it a chutt. It wasn't a chip and it wasn't a putt. So it was a chutt!

All right. Now about the longest putt ever.

I am playing in the fall tournament at Mount Anthony Country Club in Bennington, Vermont, with my brother, Jack, in a best ball match against another brother team.

We will call them Frick and Frack. Jack and I have Frick and Frack 2 down with 3 holes to go. We are playing the ninth hole, which is a short par 4 from an elevated tee. If we win the hole, we don't have to head back up the hill to 10.

That would be nice, since this will take us further from the bar.

We all hit our tee shots. Jack and Frick hit their tee shots toward the right in the rough, while Frack and I hit our drives down the middle of the fairway.

We take the carts down the hill and drop off Jack and Frick to look for their balls. Frack and I go to the fairway to hit our approach shots to the green.

Frack is about 100 yards out and he hits first. His shot is on the green and about 12 feet from the pin. I can see by the smug look on his face he thinks he has the upper hand on this hole.

I have about 90 yards to the green. I pull out my wedge and hit my shot. I chunk it and it goes about 50 yards! I now see the look on Frack's face. He really thinks he is going to win the hole. I am laying two, forty yards away and he is 12 feet away in two. He also knows that my short game isn't too good.

He's already thinking about going up the hill to number 10. I pull my cart up to my ball. Jack and Frick are still looking for their balls. I grab my long putter and get set to hit my longest chutt ever.

Now, you have to know its October in Vermont. The leaves are falling and twigs are all over the fairway. I take the putter back as far as I can and begin the descending blow. Off the ball goes, bouncing off leaves and twigs.

All I can think of is Caddy Shack and Chevy Chase putting with his eyes closed and making that funny noise while he is putting.

By now, Frack is on the green bending over to mark his ball and here comes my ball, barreling down the fairway.

This ball had radar in it. It's heading right towards the flag, and then boink! It hits the flag and drops in for a birdie three.

Frack is marking his ball and sees my ball go in. I can see the brown spot on the back of his shorts after he sees my birdie chutt drop in. People in the parking lot see the putt go in and start screaming.

Jack yells over to me, "What happened?" I yell back that I've just made a birdie and he doesn't need to find his ball.

Jack, Frick and I arrive at the green in time to watch Frack line up his birdie putt. He has to make it to keep the match going. He stands over his ball with the brown spot on the back of his pants. I know Frack has no chance of making this putt. I'm right. He doesn't even hit the hole.

After shaking hands and congratulating everyone on a good match, it's off to the bar. Frick and Frack can't wait to tell everyone how they lost the match, and Jack and I about how we won it.

And the beer really tasted great that afternoon!

CARS I HAVE OWNED

The VW Bug

I bought a 1963 VW Bug in 1973 for $300' it had a great color. I think it was called "Puke Green"

One problem with these old bugs was that you had heat or absolutely no heat.

The wires to adjust the heat were on the underside of the car, and eventually they would rust and freeze in the on or off position. I had heat all the time, and the harder I worked the engine the more heat I got. My problem was I was dating a girl who lived over the other side of Bromley Mountain. To get over that mountain I had to keep the car in third gear and rev the engine.

That would make the heat just pour out – which was okay in the winter, but not so good in the summer.

Going to her house in the summer I would try to stick one leg out the window to get a breeze into my crotch to keep my pants from getting wet with sweat to the point it looked like I wet them.

Thankfully, we stayed on that side of the mountain for our dates, so she wouldn't have to endure the heat and ride with me with one leg sticking out the window!

One night I am at a party, and I come up with a great idea to visit a girl that I had a crush on. Heading out in the Bug, I head into a sharp corner a little too fast for the car. I catch the shoulder, pull to the right, and yank it back to the left.

The Bug comes left a little too fast and decides that it wants to roll over and play dead.

But the Bug doesn't make it all the way over, so I am holding onto the steering wheel with my head on the roof, holding me up. I am able to climb out of the car, and try with my super strength to push it back over on its four wheels and drive away.

Not happening.

With the Bug in the road, I hitch a ride back to the party and grab five football players to go back with me and push the car back over so I can drive it away.

Unfortunately, the cops are there when we get back, and a tow truck is hitched to the bug, pulling it down the road, trying to get it to flip onto its wheels.

After about fifty yards and plenty of sparks, it finally flips back over. I then fill out the paperwork with the cops and go back the next morning to where the car was towed, pull the battery out, clean it up, add some water to the cells, put the battery back in, start the car and drive it away.

The roof is scratched and dented, but it is drivable.

I drive the Bug like that for a couple of months. One night I'm with three of my friends and I look down at the odometer and notice that the Bug is going to turn 55,000 miles. Not exactly a milestone, but an excuse to celebrate.

We are right in front of the entrance to the Country Club, so I pull in, just as the odometer rolls over. We jump out of the car, and the four of us start dancing on the roof. By the time we get done, the roof is collapsed and touches the tops of the front seats. We have to crawl into the car, kick and pound the roof, and try to make enough room so we can sit up without hitting our heads. After about twenty minutes, we are able to accomplish our mission. We pull out of the driveway, laughing at the thought of what we just did, thinking it was a great idea.

But, for the next month, every time we get into the car, we pound out another dent! I keep the car for a couple more of months, though, and then sell it for $100!

The ICK

At the time I was running TJ and Mike's Place III, I was approached by Point -- the -- bartender, who used to work for me in Hoosick Falls.

He borrowed the money from the register to make a bet on a sure winner that came in last.

Now, Point wants to borrow $800. I ask him what he needs the money for and he tells me he wants to buy a 1963 Buick Skylark Convertible. I tell him that I am not the bank, but if he can't get the money for the car, I will buy it for the $800 and give him $100 for his troubles.

That's how I ended up with the ICK, named by the kids because the "BU" was missing from BUICK on the front of the car. The car was in fair shape and was drive-able. As a bang around convertible, I knew I could have a great time with it. The ICK had the same problem as the Bug, though. The heat wouldn't shut off!

One time I had to drive the boys over Bromley Mountain to meet their mother half way (the same mountain I had to take the Bug over to meet my old girlfriend).

By the time we got over to the other side, though, I think RT's sneakers had melted to the carpet in the front seat! The boys begged me to never take them in that car again!

I had a customer at the time who was a professor in the Hospitality Department of local college. He asked me if I would give him a ride over to Saratoga to take a look at a restaurant that was struggling and had hired him as a consultant.

"Sure, I'll drive. Let's take the ICK!"

The ride over is no problem, and after looking at the restaurant, we head back. I pull into a Stewart's gas station to get a couple of beers for the ride back. The passenger door on the old ICK sometimes wouldn't close tight, so there I am pulling into the station making a left hand turn with the professor leaning against the passenger door.

It pops open.

The professor is in his late 60's, over weight, and not in good shape.

I watch him in what seems like slow motion, as he is falling out the door and I am trying to catch him. Unable to catch him, I watch as he lands on his ass in the middle of the gas station parking lot.

The shock on his face is crazy! I can still see it. I jam the car into park, jump out, and run around the car to help him. Luckily, we were going slow so the fall wasn't that bad. But it's still shocking.

I get him back into the car, run in to get a few beers, get back to the car and give him a cold one to settle him down. After a few minutes, he is starting to get better. I slam the door shut and proceed back to home. We stop at every bar I can find, buy the professor beers, and hope to get him drunk enough to forget the whole ordeal. It must have worked, because he never said another word about it to me.

But having said that, he never did ask me to consult on another project again.

For $800 the old ICK was fun to have. I eventually traded it for a big screen TV.

1986 Lincoln Town Car

I had a customer who was a bus driver. We called him Joe Bus. Joe came to me one day and told me his mother had passed away and he was trying to sell her car. Knowing how Joe took care of his bus, this car had to be a creampuff!

I asked Joe what type car it was and how much he wanted. He replied, "A 1986 Lincoln Town Car and $1,000 *is the asking price." I told Joe I would give him $800, sight unseen. Sold! Now I was a proud owner of a Lincoln that I had never seen! Joe dropped it off at the house and there it sat while I tried to figure out what to do with it.*

Well, at the time I was flying back and forth to Stuart, Florida, renting a car every time I got to Florida. I was in the process of trying to sell Carmody's in Stuart, so I Decided I would drive the Lincoln to Florida and leave it there so I would have a car when I flew down there.

On New Year's Day, I pull out of Bennington in my Lincoln with a major hangover. If you're going to drive 1,500 miles, there's no reason to feel good. I reach the New York Thruway 87 in Albany and head south in the Lincoln.

At 65 miles an hour I turn on the cruise control. The cruise control doesn't work! (So much for the cream puff theory.) I finally arrive in Stuart with a very stiff right leg.

While working at the bar one day, I get a phone call from my brother Jack. He needs a fourth for golf that afternoon at the Floridian. Can I play? Sure, no problem, meet you there at 12:30.

Let me tell you about the Floridian. It was owned by Wayne Huizenga! Yeah, the same guy who owned the Miami Dolphins. The Floridian had two members, Wayne and his wife. They invite another fifty or so people to be their guests, so you can see this is a very exclusive place.

You pull up to the gate and there is an intercom system. I announce TJ Carmody is here to play golf with Jack Carmody. The gate swings open. I drive down a stone paver driveway, with the shrubs carved into animals, just like Disney World. Then I come around a corner and there's a magnificent club house on the St. Lucie River.

The cart guy and caddie are waiting for me when I pull up. You should have seen their faces when this 1986 Lincoln makes the corner!

I pop the trunk, get out, tell them the keys are in the car, and don't scratch it when they park it. There is no parking lot at the Floridian. They back up the cars on the grass around the club house. There goes my Lincoln, next to a Jag, a Beemer, a Porche and a couple of cars that sell well over $100,000. At least I had the Lincoln washed on my way to the course.

We go out and play and end up back at the bar for a couple of cocktails.

When we leave, the sun has gone down, so I walk out to my car, the keys are in the door, the clubs are cleaned and in the trunk -- class all the way.

I head out after a great day at a great course, hoping to be asked back again.

A couple of weeks go by and Jack calls, and needs a fourth. I tell him I'll meet him there. He replies that he will meet me at the church a couple of miles away from Floridian. OK?

I meet Jack at the church and put my clubs into his trunk and get into his Beemer. Off we go, and I ask him why I couldn't meet him there. Jack explains to me that the 1986 Lincoln is the only car to ever leak oil on the grass at the Floridian. Mrs. H. was pissed, and they had to re-sod the grass!

So I'm allowed to play golf at the Floridian, but my car is banned!

LIVING DOWNTOWN

I was born in Bennington in 1955 when the family lived in Manchester Vermont. Shortly after I was born, we moved to 117 Union Street in Bennington. The street was right behind Main Street in Bennington, so we were right downtown.

Our view was the back of the stores that faced Main Street, so I was a downtown rat. We played on the roofs of the stores, in their parking lots, on Main Street. Downtown was ours.

Here are a few stories about growing up downtown.

The Manes Family

On the corner of Union Street and Silver Street was a very big colonial house owned by Dr. Manes and his wife. He had his office in his house and the family lived upstairs. I think both of them were under five feet tall. They were from somewhere in Europe, so they were hard to understand with their accents.

On my fifth birthday I was given a brand new sports car. Well, it was one of those old metal peddle cars. I would peddle that car up and down the street all day long. I loved that car.

One day Mrs. Manes walks down the street and knocks on our front door. Speaking in her foreign accent, Mrs. Manes tries to explain to my mother that she is going to try to get her driver's license, and since she has no experience at driving, she was wondering if she could take my peddle car out for a spin.

I'll be damned if I am going to let some forty-year-old lady take my hot little sports car out for a spin! I can just picture it now. She's cruising up and down Union Street with her hair blowing in the wind?

Thank God, my mother told her that she didn't think it would help her learn to drive a real automobile.

My Mother's Car

My father owned a used car lot when I was a kid. So you'd think my mother would have a decent car. But no! The house on Union Street had a sloped driveway and the car my mother was driving had a weak battery. In the morning my mother would let her car roll down the hill backwards into the middle of Union Street, get out of the car, open the trunk, pull out the spare tire (which was on a rope), then affix the spare tire to the bumper. Then, she'd wait for the next car to come down Union Street, flag the driver down and ask the driver to push her car so she could jump start it.

We called these crazy solutions to these problems "A Carmody Cob Job".

Another Carmody Cob Job

My father purchased some cement steps for the back door of the house on Union Street. He got a great deal. The steps lasted one winter. After putting salt to melt winter ice on these steps, they disintegrated.

My father decided then and there that he was never going to buy steps again.

In the garage was a long wooden plank. That plank was put there in place of the steps. It was about 18 inches wide and 15 feet long. It stayed there until we moved. Everyone who visited our house had to "walk the plank" to get in or out of the house.

My job was to shovel the plank in the winter. It didn't take long. I would just push the shovel down the plank and I was done. I guess if I knew better, I would have been embarrassed when friends came over to visit, but I wasn't. I just knew it was another Carmody Cob Job!

Carmody's Theatre

My mother taught dance, so in the garage she had all the props that she would use for her shows. My sister Patty and a couple of the other kids in the neighborhood would put on a show every once in a while, using those props.

We would go up and down Union Street selling tickets to the shows for a quarter, which was a lot of money back then.

On a Saturday we would have seats set up, a sheet for the curtain, and all the props ready to go. All the neighbors would show up to get their quarter's worth. We would do songs like: "If you knew Suzy like I knew Suzy", dumb skits, and whatever else we could come up with to entertain the ten people who would show up.

With $2.50 taken in we thought we were rich! Ed Mahar would always show up for the show. Ed owned the funeral home where I would eventually work. Ed would give us $10. Holy shit! Pay dirt! We would go out for burger and fries that night -- on Ed.

The Battle Monument

Bennington has a battle monument built to recognize a famous battle in the Revolutionary War against the British. I think it is the second largest monument in the USA, second only to the one in Washington.

The Monument has an elevator that you can take to the observation floor, where you can see three states, New York, Vermont, and Massachusetts. There are only two buttons in the elevator, one for up and one for down.

Fall foliage is a busy time in Bennington with a lot leaf peepers checking out the scenery. On a Saturday or Sunday, my sister Patty and I would position ourselves in the elevator right next to the two buttons. When the peepers would get on the elevator we would charge them 25 cents for the ride.

How could you turn down two adorable kids?

Patty and I would do this until we made enough money to get lunch or candy. The amazing thing is that we never got caught

Story #34

BIRTHDAYS!

September 16, 1955, Marguerite Carmody goes into labor in Manchester, Vermont. John T. Carmody Sr. is in Rutland, 30 miles away, playing poker at the Elks Club. Fifteen year old John T. Carmody Jr. is sitting in the car waiting to drive his mother 30 miles to the Putnam Memorial Hospital in Bennington.

Somehow, JT Sr. is notified that his wife has gone into to labor. He flies out of the Elks and exceeds the speed limit on Route 7, from Rutland to Manchester.

He pulls into the driveway as Marguerite is getting into the car with her fifteen year old son behind the wheel. He's ready to make his first trip driving to Bennington.

Out of the seat goes J.T. Jr.

Into the seat goes J.T. Sr., and off the car goes to Bennington.

Sometime later, there is a cry in the delivery room at the Putnam Memorial Hospital. A little black baby is born. Well, he was black because the umbilical cord was wrapped around his neck.

That baby immediately knew what a cruel world it was going to be. Thomas Joseph Carmody born September 17 at 4:12 AM to Marguerite Loveday Carmody and John T. Carmody Sr. The fifth child and the third boy.

I am sure I had great birthday parties as I grew up, but there are a few I remember more than others.

The 18th Birthday

I was one of the youngest in my class to graduate from high school in 1973. I had to wait until the end of the summer before it was legal for me to drink in the bars.

Of course, that didn't stop me. All summer long I drank at a little bar called The Taco House. Their motto was "Over a million tacos served nationally. Over one taco served here!"

The barmaid was a friendly older lady named Charlotte. She took care of me all summer. Even back then I was a generous tipper. Well, the day finally arrives: Sept. 17, 1973. I head off to The Taco House to celebrate my 18th birthday.

As I walk into the Taco House, Charlotte is coming around the bar, and heading towards me. She grabs my arm and says we need to talk. Out the door we go. She informs me that she has been told by one of the other customers that I am not eighteen and that I am not allowed in the bar.

I look at Charlotte with a big smile and tell her today is my birthday. Well now, it's old home week. Charlotte can't be happier. Back we go into the Taco House to celebrate!

I should be able to remember what I did for my 21st birthday, but I don't.

I had graduated from Hudson Valley Community College and was working at the funeral home full-time. I am sure I celebrated it at the In Town Bar.

30th Birthday, September 17, 1985

It's at Danny's West Coral Springs Florida: I am the manager at Danny's and I come up with a great idea!

"Let's do a "Half-Way to St. Patrick's Day Party."

I approach Danny and tell him about my idea. He doesn't think it's a good idea. He does so well on St. Pat's Day that he doesn't want the customers to feel they are being milked with another St. Pat's party.

I hesitate for a minute, and then I tell him, "Let's do a "Surprise 30th Birthday and Half-Way to St. Pat's Party!"

He asks me whose birthday it is, and I tell him it is mine. He thinks it's a great idea. We set up the party, get bagpipers, a band, the green beer and corned beef and cabbage.

The party is awesome. As far as I know it was the first half-way to St. Patrick's Day party in Fort Lauderdale.

40th Birthday, September 17, 1995

I am a partner at TJ and Mikes Place III in North Bennington, Vermont. I put on another half-way to St. Pat's Day plus TJ's birthday party.

We have a great time. After most everyone has gone, a couple of us are still sitting at the bar. One of the customers says he has a hot tub at his house about a mile away. He says we ought to go there and get in the tub and have a few more cocktails.

Great idea, let's go!

After a few more drinks and about an hour later, everyone leaves and I pass out at this guy's house.

Waking up in the middle of the night, I can't find the bathroom, so I stumble around the house looking for the bathroom. I get the funny feeling I have been here before. When I wake up the next morning I tell the guy that I think I have been here before. He tells me I must be mistaken.

But when we are backing out of the driveway, I look up and recognize the house. My sister, Patty, and her husband had the house built a few years earlier.

50th Birthday, September 17, 2005

We're at Carmody's Downtown in Bennington, Vermont. It's going to be my 50th birthday and it's going to be a big party.

I have three days of festivities planned. A golf tournament on Friday, a Friday night cocktail party at my brother Jack's house, a Half-Way to St. Patrick's Day

Party on Saturday night at Carmody's Downtown, and a Sunday Brunch at my house.

On Thursday night, I pull out the big green bus and head over to the Albany airport. About fifteen people are flying up from Stuart, Florida, for the party. I don't have a license to drive the bus. Who cares? I own it, and I am going to drive it!

Well, the group gets off the plane and they are all wearing T shirts with "Airfare: $300. Drinks: $50. Food: $25. T.J.'s Birthday Party: Priceless. I can't believe they don't have a shirt for me!

We get everybody on the bus and I head to the first bar I can find and we work our way to Bennington from there.

On Friday we have the golf tournament. It is highlighted by my nephew making eagle on 15 and 16 at Taconic.

Friday night is the cocktail party at Jack's house. It's supposed to be from 6 to 8, but obviously goes longer than that. In the middle of the party they carry out a casket. In the casket is one of my good friends dressed like me and wearing a TJ mask. About 10p.m. the police show up at the house on a noise complaint. Jack's wife thinks they are strippers for my birthday.

They close us down, but by then the party is winding down and everyone is heading to Downtown to finish out the night.

For my birthday I have a hundred T-shirts made up with a picture of me doing the Irish jig. On the shirt was printing, "I was with TJ when he jigged his way thru the big 5 0."

I told RT and Patrick that we need to sell fifty shirts to break even, I have a tendency to have a few cocktails and give away the shirts. So I figure I will give away half and try to sell the other half to break even.

Saturday is the big day, and the 17th falls right on that day. You couldn't ask for a better party.

We are packed. We have a piper, a band, corned beef and green beer. I'm up and down from the top of the bar singing Irish songs too many times to count.

If you didn't have a good time that night you were probably dead.

Sunday is brunch at my house. Just what we needed after three days of hard partying. Plenty of mimosas and Bloody Marys. I think I got around eight bottles of Johnny Walker Blue.

About 3 p.m. it winds down. I get the bus and drive the Florida crew back to the airport, and return back to Bennington to detox for the next couple of days. On Monday morning, I get to my office and get ready to do the paper work from the weekend. The first thing I want to check are the T-shirt sales, praying that we were able to sell 50 shirts. All 100 shirts are gone and there is only $30.00 in the T-shirt bag.

Not bad. I gave away 97 T-shirts.

With my 60th birthday approaching I told Sue I just wanted to go out to dinner, just the two of us. I knew that wasn't going to happen! My sister-in-law Kathy set up a little party with my nieces and nephews showing up and a few other close friends. It was a nice quiet party for a change.

I think, though, if I live to be 70, I will throw myself just one more good birthday bash!

THE FAMILY TREE!

The Family Tree

My mother always said we were of Irish decent. So one day I am hosting for lunch at Carmody's Downtown, and this fellow comes in and asks for the owner. I tell him I am the owner. Well, he says that he's my cousin.

My reply is that everyone says that because they want a free drink.

"No! No!" he says. "I really am your cousin. Your grandmother's name was Agnes."

I think, "No shit! He really does know something about the family."

We talk for a while and I find out he is from Connecticut. He's been doing some research on the family tree. Before he leaves, I load him up with Carmody's root beer, glasses, hats, and t-shirts. He promises to send me all the research he has done.

A couple of weeks later a manila envelope arrives at the restaurant, I open it up and there is the family tree.

Here is what the first page says:

Descendants of John Carmody
Generation No. 1

John Carmody was born October 7, 1828 in Adare, County Limerick, Ireland, and died September 29, 1888 two miles outside of Poultney, Vermont, while returning to Granville, New York. He married Margaret Brearton. She was born May 10, 1836, in County Kilkenny, Ireland, and died July 14, 1908 in Rutland, Vermont.

Notes for John Carmody:
Died as a result of a fall from a wagon. (Poultney Death Records v.2., p.165, 1.47)

Article in Granville Sentinel-October 5, 1888:

"Death in the Darkness"
"SATURDAY'S FATAL ACCIDENT
ON A COUNTRY ROAD
"Two teams meet and the result is John Carmody was thrown to the ground and almost instantly expires-The Largely Attended Obsequies.

"Saturday evening was one of intense darkness. The glimmering satellites of the heavens were veiled by heavy, somber clouds.
"The streets and highways were rendered dangerous to travelers. It was on this night that two teams going slowly in opposite directions collided on a Hampton Road.

"An occupant of one of the vehicles thrown to the ground and a few minutes later a spirit passed from its tenement of clay up through the overhanging bank of darkness to dwell with the legions beyond the stars.

"A HIGHLY RESPECTED MAN"

"The life which so suddenly went out was that of John Carmody who resided at New Boston just over the Vermont line and a short distance from this village. The deceased had been to Fair Haven visiting a brother, James, who was returning with him. They proceeded very slowly, owing to extreme darkness to within two miles of Poultney, and, when near the residence of John Ray, collided with a team going in the opposite direction as already stated. This team proved to be on driven by Gardner Parker, a well-known slate manufacturer, who was also driving in a slow cautious manner.

"Although the shock was not a severe one, it was sufficient to throw Mr. Carmody to the ground. It is probable that he was leaning forward in an endeavor to see the road track.

"His skull was fractured by the fall and death shortly ensued. It is impossible to determine whether the fracture was caused by coming in contact with a stone or by a kick from the horse.

"A LARGE FUNERAL

"The deceased was sixty-years-old, and is survived by a widow and four grownup daughters and two sons. He married a sister of Matthew Brayton, and was uncle of Mrs. John Heffernan of this place. The deceased was a resident of Granville some twenty-five years ago. The funeral was held from the house Tuesday fore noon, requiem high mass being celebrated at the Middle Granville Catholic Church, the Reverend Father Hayden officiating. The esteem in which the deceased was held was shown by the fact that the funeral procession numbered 110 vehicles.

"More about John Carmody:
"Burial: Mount Carmel Cemetery, Granville, NY
"Notes for Margaret Brearton:
"aka Brayton, Breareton (PHS p. 1452 marriage record)

"Living with her daughter Alice Haugh when she died.

As you can see, my great great grandfather was killed in a wagon accident in October, 1888. Not thinking about it very much, a couple of years later I read a book about how the Irish came to Vermont.

In the book they tell you the most of them came through Montréal because it was easier than Ellis Island. When they got into Vermont they went to work in the marble and slate quarries. It was back-breaking work and the only employment the Irish could get. While reading the book I come across a little tidbit that back then Vermont was a dry state.

Then it hits me! I pull the family tree and read the article about the death of my great great grandfather.

Okay, here is where I do my best Inspector Jacques Clouseau impression:

1. It's late at night. Why would anyone be traveling in a wagon so late, especially you don't have head lights?

2. The article says there were 110 vehicles in the funeral procession. Yes, 110 vehicles in 1888!

3. My great-great-grand father was a bootlegger!

It was late at night. He and his brother were returning to Granville, New York after making a delivery to Poultney, Vermont.

4. Everyone likes an Irish wake, because they know it is going to be a great party. But 110 vehicles? If you are going to go to an Irish wake, wouldn't you want to go to one where the deceased was a bootlegger and there was a guarantee they wouldn't run out of booze?

5. Now, this gets me thinking, which is sometimes scary.

If my great-great-grandfather hadn't died, the Carmody clan could be as powerful as the Kennedy clan. After all, JFK's father made his millions selling Scotch.

Shit, I could have been President!

SAVANNAH PERCHANCE

While attending Hudson Valley Community College for mortuary science, I got to meet some real characters!

Most students get into the business by having their family in the business, but you get some who, on a whim, decide they want to be funeral directors.

I'm not sure if I would have chosen the funeral business if I didn't have family in it, but who am I to judge?

Anyway, on to Savannah Perchance.

In my senior year at HVCC I shared an apartment with another student, so in September, we're moving into the apartment. I soon realize I have another roommate -- Savannah Perchance.

Savannah is a little older than us. I think she was born in 1917 and unfortunately died in 1958. You see, Savannah is a tomb stone. I find out my roommate was given the headstone by a couple of his friends a couple of nights before he was heading back to Troy for our senior year.

When our senior year was over, I was given Savannah as a going away present. Taking Savannah to Bennington, I gave her a prominent spot in my new apartment. I decided that Savannah should become part of the family. I got a bra, a pair of panties and some nice heels for her. All dressed up, I'd say that Savannah looked great.

We threw her two parties a year. One was on her birthday, and the other one was on the day she died. I would invite everyone over to party, with Savannah imbibing in a few herself!

We had a little song we sang to Savannah on her two days -- "Savannah Perchance! She couldn't boogie, but she really knew how to dance!"

The story does have a happy ending! One day we had a funeral director from out of town who came to Bennington. I found out he was from the same area as Savannah, so I asked him if he would take the stone back with him and return it to the cemetery for me.

He gladly took Savannah back with him. I knew she was going to miss her yearly parties and the warmth of my nice apartment, but I felt good about getting Savannah back where she belonged.

Hearts and Vines:

The Southern Vermont Medical Center in Bennington had fund raisers which they put on every year to raise money for the hospital. It was called Hearts and Vines. It was held at the Equinox Hotel in Manchester, Vermont.

The Equinox was built 1853 and had many a famous guest Presidents Taft, Grant, and Theodore Roosevelt to name a few.

President Abraham Lincoln's wife, Mary, and her two sons visited in the summer of 1864. She enjoyed it so much she made reservations to visit the following year with the president. A special suite was built in anticipation of President Lincoln's visit.

Unfortunately, he was assassinated on April 14th in 1865.

Enough history!

So, the Ball was held there every year. The hotel would give a good rate to the guests who were going to the Ball. Sue and I took advantage of the opportunity to stay at the inn and not worry about driving home. Knowing that the Hotel would give last call for alcohol early, I would stock my room with a few libations for my friends, who didn't want the night to end so early.

The first year Sue and I check in we have a nice room, nothing fancy, and we have a few people come to the room for cocktails. A good time is had by all. When checking out, I am taken care of by a good customer of Carmody's at the front desk. She asks how everything was and I reply it was great. She asks me if we will back next year, and I tell her we will. She looks at me and tells me she will make sure that I have a great room next year.

Well, for a bunch of years, we stay in the best rooms, suites, two floor units, and every year the party in my room gets bigger. After a couple of years Equinox does some renovations and turns a former guest shop into a unit. For the next three years I get this room. When I pull up, the bellhops know me by my first name and roll down the luggage carts to move the booze and food.

Now, my room is open from the time the Ball starts until I think it is time to go to bed around 3 a.m. I stock the room with plenty of booze.The unit has a kitchen, so I also supply plenty of food, especially when we get the late night munchies.

Heading up for our fourth year, when I get the out of the car the bellhops inform me that my usual room is not available. The hotel owners saw how busy my room was during the Ball so they decided to build their own bar there. The bastards, I thought in my mind when I went in for a drink to check it out. Why? Because I had to pay for the damn drink!

That year at the Ball we were having a great time, and the band decides that they are done. I go to four of the couples we are with and convince them that we should come up with $50 a piece and have the band play for another hour. Everyone agrees and I convince the band to stay.

Working up a sweat dancing on the table, I decide to buy some drinks. I get what I call "Super Finger" every once in a while. That's where I start pointing to everyone saying, "Get them a drink!"

Well, I start "Super Finger" and start buying drinks for everyone. A grand time was had by all.

The next morning I am not sure I paid my bar tab, so on my way to brunch I stop in at the bar and luckily the bartender who was working the night before was setting up the bar. I asked him if the bar bill was all set and did I take good care of him. He responded in the affirmative.

Awesome! Off to brunch and a well-deserved mimosa.

A week later I am sitting at my desk when the phone rings. It's the accounting office at Equinox. They tell me that I have a bar tab from the Ball. I reply that I don't think I do, that I checked with the bartender and he said everything was taken care of. The accountant replies that whoever's tab it is they had a good time.

On the bill are 20 Grand Mariners. Shit! I say that has to be my tab! She tells me that, unfortunately, the bartender put the bill on the wrong room and I checked out before they had a chance to rectify the situation.

Okay, I will give you a credit card number. Then she says, "Mr. Carmody, I have another thing to tell you."

Oh boy, what's next?

"Well Mr. Carmody you asked the band to stay and play for another hour, and they never got their money!"

Shit! You got be kidding me! "No Mr. Carmody."

Well, it cost me $500, but made for a great time and a great story!

You Don't Mess Around With T!

In the 70's, one of my favorite singers was Jim Croce. One of his hits was a song called "You don't mess around with Jim."

The refrain was:

You don't tug on Superman's cape
You don't spit into the wind
You don't pull the mask off the old Lone Ranger
And you don't mess around with Jim.

Well one night at the Bar and Hibachi, doing my 50 cent drinks, with a packed bar, the song comes on! Singing it to my customers, I change the lyrics a bit:

You don't tug on Superman's cape
You don't pee in the sea
You don't pull the mask off the old lone ranger
And you don't mess around with T.

And there you have it. An instant hit!

Story #37+++

WHERE IS THE GAS?

(and a few last little things)

When I owned the bar in Hoosick Falls, I rented a house on Polock Hill. I lived there for about eight months. I had my two boys over some weekends, and I had a room for each of them.

It's a gray and windy weekend in the great Northeast. The boys have been at the bar with me while I do paperwork from Friday night. Usually, I would get lunch for them, but I think it would be a nice treat to make macaroni and cheese. I buy all the provisions for our afternoon meal.

I put the boys in front of the television while I go to the kitchen to prepare a gourmet meal from a box. I turn on the gas stove, and nothing happens. I try to relight the pilot light and that doesn't work. Now, I'm pissed!

I know the guys who own the gas company fairly well, so I give them a call, ready to ream them a new butt for letting me run out of gas. When they pick up the phone, I explain the situation as calmly as I can, and tell them I'm not very happy.

Their response is, "T. J., we took the tank out six months ago." Now, I'm the fool and it shows how much I cook at home.

Okay boys, let's go out for lunch!

Bennington Battle Monument

The Bennington Battle Monument was deducted in 1891 to commemorate the Battle of Bennington, which occurred on August 16, 1777, in nearby Hoosick, New York. The monument is 306 feet tall and is the tallest structure in Vermont. The unsuccessful objective of the British was to capture supplies in Bennington, and the battle is considered to be a turning point of the Revolutionary War.

My sister Patty and I used to sneak up there and charge the tourists $.25 to take the elevator to the top of the monument. Here's another story about that monument.

A Bennington fundraiser was held for a few years. About ten people would raise funds for the privilege of sleeping in the observation room near the top of the monument. One year, I am one of the ten fundraisers.

I go about raising as much money as I can.

On a Friday in the fall, there's a press conference and cocktail party to kick-off the overnight stay.

They dress us up in footed pajamas, take our picture, and send us to the top of the monument. I sneak away and go to work at my restaurant. I am not going to miss working on Friday night during the fall foliage season. Around 9:00 p.m. I head over to the monument, take the elevator to the observation deck, and observe the most boring party ever. The only libation they have is some kind of funky drink.

After a few minutes, I announce that I am going back to my bar for a few cocktails. Five of the nine decide to come with me, and we leave four sticks in the mud behind. We go to the bar and close it down. Back to the monument we go where the sticks in the mud are asleep. We rouse them and party until 4:00 a.m. with some good supplies from the bar. Finally, everyone falls asleep, except me.

Above the observation deck is another floor which no one gets to see, except the maintenance crew. In the inebriated state I am in, I think it would be a good idea for me to go where no man has gone before … other than the maintenance crew.

A gate guards the stairs to the next level. In much better shape than I am now, I jump the gate!

I go up the stairs and enter a big room with nothing in it but a ladder mounted to the wall. It takes the climber to the top of the monument, about 40 feet straight up. I think this is great. I will be one of the few who has made it to the top of the Bennington Battle Monument.

I begin my ascent.

About eight rungs into the climb, my foot slips and I begin to fall. Luckily, I grab hold of a rung to stop my fall. As I stand there on the rung I think what a stupid Irishman I am. If I had fallen, no one would have heard me. They are all passed out. I have gone higher than most in the monument, so it would be better to get my ass back to firm seating.

I go down slowly and thank God for keeping me safe. I jump the gate again, find my cot, and pass out cold.

Around 6:30 a.m., a committee comes to bring us breakfast. They can't get anyone to move. Everyone is still passed out. For some reason, our visitors are upset. Finally, they get us up. I pass on the breakfast and head straight home. The fundraiser was never held again.

Junior and Senior Year

In my junior year, I was a starting guard on the varsity basketball team. We were having a tough year, so our interest in the game began to wane. We began to party a little, and that was against the rules.

After one particular loss, we had a snow day. I get the keys to the gym and call a couple of teammates to come for a pick-up game. One of the players sneaks in some beer. So, in between our pick-up games, we go to the locker room to have a beer or two. Wouldn't you know ... the coach shows up. He doesn't let on that he knows we are drinking until the following day when I get called to his office where he asks me if I drank any beer yesterday.

I could have lied, but didn't. I got removed from the team with my friend who brought the beer to the gym.

Waiting to tell my father was one of the longest days of my life. It's the only time I remember him hitting me.

I survived that situation and got through the rest of my junior year. My sister Patty tells me that it might be a good idea if I ran for the vice president's office in the Student Council. She says it would look good on my transcript.

I ask, "What's a transcript and what does a Vice President do?" She explains it all to me and that a VP doesn't do anything but show up at meetings. That's good because I'm good at doing nothing. If you saw any of my transcripts, you would understand. In school, I was only as smart as the girl seated in front of me, and that was only if she moved her arm so I could read the answers.

I won the election and couldn't wait to head into my senior year ... but that's another story.

The Beginning

I don't know if having my gums rubbed for a toothache with Black Velvet when I was a baby was the start of my -- as the Irish say -- "the love for liquor."

It might have started when, as an altar boy, I decided I should taste the wine before Mass. I didn't want the priest served any wine before its time, so I sampled it to be sure it was of the right vintage.

The first time I ever drank more than a sip was in the 8th grade, when my buddies and I stumbled upon a couples cases of beer in the Little League park. I don't know who left it or why, but we felt it was our obligation to take off with it. It took a couple of weeks to finish off both cases. None went to waste. Every once in a while I will have a beer and the memory of the first bottle of beer comes back to me.

In my freshman year of high school, we moved from Bennington to Manchester, Vermont. The high school there was Burr and Burton Seminary, now known as Burr and Burton Academy. That's where I learned to party.

My first bar experience was in nearby Granville, New York. I get a ride over with a senior and another kid who was a junior. I was a sophomore. We go into this bar and sit right at the bar. The bartender asks us what we are drinking. We all order beers. She never asks us for ID's.

So there we are, drinking and having a good time, when the senior who's with us decides to speak up ... and says he is only 17. Well, the junior in our trio says he's only 16, and then I profess proudly that I am only 15! We are promptly escorted out the door, but there a plenty more trips to Granville.

HOT TUB ON WHEELS!!!

In 1992 I owned a bar in Hoosick Falls NY called T.J. O'Carmodys (I guess I didn't think Carmody was Irish enough, so I threw in the 'O' for good measure).

The bar was in a town close to the Vermont border and had a 4 o'clock license, so you can imagine the crazies that came thru there.

When I leased the bar there was a vacant lot across the street, owned by the railroad. So I had the great idea of buying the land and putting in two volley ball courts. My negotiations with the railroad went like this:

Me: "How much do you want for the vacant lot?"

Railroad: "$25,000"

Me: "Would you take $20,000?"

Rail road: "Kid we are the railroad. We don't care if we sell it or not, so come up with the $25,000 or leave us alone.

What a great negotiator I was!

Having leagues four nights a week really helped increase the business from May to October. On some weekends I would run volley ball tournaments to benefit local charities.

One weekend I ran a tournament to benefit Big Brothers and Big Sisters. The tournament was a co-ed tournament and would start at 8 a.m. Saturday morning, with round robin play, and continue to around 8 p.m. Saturday night. It would start again Sunday morning and finish up Sunday at 5 p.m.

On Saturday afternoon the weather was brutally hot, so I contacted one of doormen, who had a business called Hot Tub on Wheels.

It was a six-person hot tub on a trailer that he would take to your house for the weekend or a night, set it up, put the heat on, and you had a hot tub for the weekend. His main business was during the winter, so his tub was available for the weekend. I asked him to bring it down to the bar and set it up, minus the heat.

Well the tub was a hit for the volleyball players! They could jump in and cool off between games.

The weekend went great. Business was good, the weather was great, and the tournament was a success.

So Sunday around 5:30 p.m., we presented the winning team with their trophies, and gave BB/BS their money from the tournament.

I decided at that point, it was time for me to have a nice big scotch and relax in the hot tub.

As I said, the hot tub was built for six people. When I got out side with my cocktail, there were about 10 people hanging in the hot tub.

Well ... there is always room for one more, so I was able to get my feet into the tub and sit on the side enjoying my beverage, admiring a couple of the women volley ball players who had been smart enough to bring a bathing suit for the occasion.

As I was relaxing, Ray -- the owner of the hot tub -- came up to me and asked if I would like to go for a ride. I looked at him like he was crazy and said, "Why would I want to go for a ride while I am enjoying my cocktail and the scenery?

Ray reply was, "Let's take the hot tub for a ride."

I asked, "With all these people in the tub?"

Ray goes, "Sure!"

And he proceeds to back his truck up to the trailer. Well, everyone makes sure they have a full beverage for the ride, and off we go down the little side street that the bar was on, and then, making a right onto one of the main streets in town.

Everyone is having a great time! Water is splashing, drinks are flowing. We're waving to bystanders on the side walk!

What a grand old time, until one of the town police patrols comes the other way and goes by us.

The look on his face was priceless, but I knew it wasn't going to be good for us.

So while the officer is trying to do a U-turn, Ray is stepping on the gas, trying to get us back to the bar by making a right onto a side street and another right on another one, which brought us back to the bar.

Well, Inspector Closeau could find us. All he had to do was follow the spilled water that was in the middle of the road.

So the officer finally pulled us over on the second side street.

As he is approaching the hot tub, I'm telling everyone to put their drinks under water, hoping he would not notice (yeah, no chance!).

Well the officer walks right by the hot tub and approaches Ray, the driver.

While the two of them are talking, I am figuring out in my head how much this is going to cost me.

Let's see: 10 people with open containers @ $50 a piece! That's $500, and whatever else the officer can come up with.

Like I said, I had a good weekend and had some money in the safe, but this isn't how I had imagined I was going to spend it.

So everyone was on pins and needles, watching the officer and Ray have their conversation. Ray used to be on the police force, so I was hoping this might be a plus for me!

After about five minutes, the officer leaves Ray and approaches the hot tub. Thank God everyone is on good behavior and not saying anything to the officer.

He approaches me and says, "Mr. Carmody. Do you know why I stopped this hot tub on wheels?"

My answer was, "No officer. I don't know why we were stopped."

His reply was -- and I will remember it 'til the day I die -- "I wanted to make sure that everyone had their seatbelts on. Now get this hot tub back to the bar and if you move it again today, I will arrest your ass!"

Me? I said, 'Thank you officer. I guarantee it will not move again!"

Well, Ray got us back to the bar and the hot tub didn't move again that night, but the cocktails flowed and the story was told over and over!

Not everyone can say they got pulled over in a hot tub!

Greatest
St. Patrick's Day ever!

March 17, 2018 was the greatest St. Pat's day for me!

You've read all about my escapades on St. Pats Day, from singing on the bar to starting parades. I have had some great times, but 2018 was the best ever. For the first time ever, I was able to spend the day without myself or my four boys having to work it. We spent it at McGrath's Pub at the Inn at Long Trail on top of Mendon Mountain in Vermont.

I flew up from Florida. Jeff flew in from Denver. It was going to be his bachelor party weekend. RT and Patrick picked us up in Albany along with Jeff's good friend and a former Carmody's employee, Austin, who flew in from Jackson Hole, Wyoming.

After spending Wednesday night in Bennington, the boys got up and did some skiing at Mount Snow. Then, we headed to Rutland -- to party central -- which turns out to be Ryan's house.

Thursday night we ordered pizza. Krissy, my daughter in law, and the two grandchildren -- Addison and Mera -- joined us. After a few cocktails, some great stories and a crazy card game called Cards Against Humanity, we called it a night.

The boys went skiing at Killington in the morning and I took Krissy and the girls out for breakfast before they headed out to her mother's house, so she could get as far away as possible from this bachelor party.

I met the boys at a bar on the mountain after skiing. No skiing for me. The doctor told me that if I fell, I could hurt the baby. There were eight of us for dinner that night and we had a great time. We ended up at the Elks for some shuffle board. Every one stayed pretty good knowing that Saturday was going to be a long day.

The boys went skiing again in the morning, but got home in time to be ready to head to the bar at 2 p.m. for the St. Patrick's Day festivities. We had a van pick us up: RT, Patrick, Ryan, Jeff, Austin, Greg and myself.

We arrived at the Pub on top of the mountain. I nearly froze my ass off while Patrick snapped a picture of me by a 10 foot-tall snow bank. That was the longest amount of time I spent outside the whole trip.

The Pub was packed and the band was playing some great pub songs. As we worked our way down the full bar we were able to order seven pints of Guinness. I know my way around a bar, so within 45 minutes we had seats and control of half the bar. We stayed for the next six hours. Plenty of Guinness, some singing, and meeting some great people at the bar.

I couldn't have been more proud, enjoying my favorite day with my boys, some old friends and some new friends. We got picked up by the van and ended the night at the Elks with some corned beef and cabbage and more shuffle board.

On Sunday, everyone headed back home, with smiles on their faces, knowing they had spent some great time with family.

This is my last story for this book! I hope you enjoyed it as much as I have writing it. Life is full of ups and downs, and I have had my share. But I consider myself a very blessed man with the family and friends I have.

As I always said when someone was leaving one of my bars: May the Lord be with you! And be with you too!

###

Made in the USA
Columbia, SC
19 February 2023

12506688R00113